Building a roadmap to success.

The Growth Matrix

A Strategic Blueprint for Future-Driven Business Growth and Success

By **Rajalingam Rathinam**

Copyright © 2023 Rajalingam Rathinam. All rights reserved.

No part of this book may be reproduced or transmitted in any form or by any means, electronic or mechanical, including photocopying, recording, or any information storage and retrieval system, without prior written permission from the author, except for the inclusion of brief quotations in a review.

The examples and case studies used in this book are based on the author's research and experience and are not provided by the companies. While every effort has been made to ensure the accuracy of the information presented, the author and publisher make no warranties or representations as to the accuracy, completeness, or reliability of such information. The author and publisher disclaim any liability, loss, or risk incurred as a consequence, directly or indirectly, of the use and application of any of the contents of this book.

ISBN: 979-83-8825-009-4

Published by: Aberame, India | Australia

Cover design & Interior Layout by: Rajalingam Rathinam

Printed in: April 2023

Any additional legal notices or permissions required by law or the terms of the book's publication should also be included on the copyright page.

My family has been the foundation of my life's journey. Your unwavering support and love have made me who I am today, and forever grateful. This book is a tribute to you and a testament to the power of family in shaping our successes and failures.

Acknowledgment

I want to express my deepest gratitude to the society that has sculpted me into who I am today. It takes a village to raise a child, and I am a product of the collective efforts of all the people who have supported me throughout my life.

While I often refer to myself as a self-made professional, I must acknowledge that it is only through the lessons I have learned from the people who have ditched me and the failures that I have experienced that I have been able to chart a successful path for myself. I am truly grateful for all these experiences, as they have shaped me into who I am today.

I express my heartfelt gratitude to my wife and daughter, who have been my pillars of strength and support throughout the writing of this book. Their unwavering encouragement and support have been instrumental in helping me to bring this project to fruition.

I am deeply indebted to my mother, from whom I have inherited my tenacity and resilience, and to the memory of my father, grandmother, and grandfather, who have always been my guiding lights.

I want to express my sincere appreciation to all the friends, colleagues, clients, vendors, suppliers, partners, and guides who have provided me with invaluable feedback and encouragement throughout the writing of this book. I am particularly grateful to my friend Rajesh Vairapandian, a constant source of motivation and inspiration, urging me to set and pursue goals with determination.

And, my heartfelt gratitude to my teachers, C.S. Yogarajan and S. Madasamy, who ignited my talent and helped me develop the skills and knowledge necessary to succeed professionally.

I owe a debt of gratitude to my first boss, V. Rajendran, who provided me with my first professional opportunity and helped me to develop the skills and experience necessary to succeed in the corporate world. I am also indebted to my mentor, G. Prabagar, for their unwavering support and guidance throughout my career.

My deep appreciation for Pat Flynn, SPI Media, and the many books that have provided me with invaluable guidance and inspiration throughout my journey. It is only through the collective efforts of all these people that I have been able to write this book on organizational growth, and I am genuinely grateful to every one of them.

In addition to the people I have already mentioned, I also want to express my gratitude to the many other individuals who have played a role in helping me to bring this book to fruition.

I thank the editors, publishers, and printers who have worked tirelessly to bring this book to life. I also acknowledge the importance of design and layout in creating a visually appealing and engaging book. As this book's designer and layout artist, I take pride in contributing to its visual impact and overall success.

I am grateful to the organizations and companies to which I can relate my strategies well and to examples to illustrate the concepts and strategies outlined in this book. Without their support and cooperation, this book would not have been possible.

Furthermore, I must acknowledge the support of my more comprehensive network, including industry associations, professional organizations, and online communities, who have provided me with valuable insights, feedback, and support throughout the writing process.

Last but not least, I want to express my appreciation to all the readers who will pick up this book and engage with its ideas. This book will provide the insights and tools you need to drive growth and success within your organizations.

Contents

Acknowledgment 4
Contents 7
Preface 9
Introduction 15
Organization Growth 19
Branding & Marketing for Growth 27
Sales for Growth 37
Building Customer Relationships for Growth 51
Nurturing Employee Well-being for Growth 61
Innovation for Growth 71
Diversification for Growth 85
Digital Transformation for Growth 99
Financial Management for Growth 113
Collaboration and Partnership for Growth 127
Continuous Improvement for Growth 139
Training and Development for Growth 151
Data-Driven Decision for Growth 163
Sustainable Business Practice for Growth 175
Global Expansion for Growth 189
Mergers and Acquisitions for Growth 199
Conclusion 209
Sources & References 217
About Author 218

Preface

It was a typical Hong Kong evening, cool and breezy, and I was returning to my hotel room after a long and tiring brainstorming session with a client. As I stepped onto the MTR, a wave of relief washed over me as I observed the unusual spaciousness of the train. My journey from Kowloon Bay to Central required a transfer from the Green Line to the Red Line at Yau Ma Tei station. I made my way to a seat near the entrance and took a moment to bask in the rare opportunity for relaxation, closing my eyes to unwind fully.

That's when I noticed a European sitting next to me, exchanged greetings, and went back to my reverie. However, it was only a short time before the gentleman beside me started talking to the girl he was traveling with. He was speaking rather loudly about his startup, which was growing alarmingly. The investors were pressuring him for higher returns, and he had to focus on organizational growth to keep up. His companion seemed skeptical and tried to voice something, but he was determined to do it.

I consciously tried not to interrupt their conversation and instead chose to listen in, even though I knew it wasn't the best thing to do. While eavesdropping is not ideal, the situation compelled me to do so. Finally, the MTR reached Mong Kok and realized I needed to get off at Yau Ma Tei for a change to the red line. I debated introducing myself to the gentleman before I left but ultimately decided against it. However, as the train approached Yau Ma Tei, I changed my mind and quickly handed him my business card, telling him to contact me if he needed help with his growth strategy.

The gentleman looked slightly taken aback but nodded in acknowledgment as I exited the train. After that, I forgot about the incident and went about my business.

A few days later, I received a message on WeChat from the same gentleman, inviting me for dinner to discuss his startup's growth strategy. He introduced himself as Martin Castro, a Spanish expatriate who had launched a restaurant booking aggregator app with his girlfriend, Shyamala, from Singapore. The startup had already secured an angel investor and wanted to expand further.

I agreed to meet with Martin and Shyamala at Oolaa Central on Stanley Street, and we started our conversation. Unfortunately, as they explained their issues and requirements, I got lost in their startup's potential.

Martin and Shyamala were very calculated in their plans, which impressed me. Moreover, they were even getting married the following year, which made the situation even more dramatic.

As we talked, I found myself getting more and more invested in their startup's success. It was like I had stumbled onto a hidden gem and was determined to help them achieve their goals.

We talked late into the night, discussing growth strategies and potential investors. By the end of it, Martin and Shyamala were beaming with excitement. They were grateful for my help and eager to get started.

As we parted ways, I wondered how a chance encounter on the MTR could lead to such an exciting opportunity. In the end, Martin and Shyamala's startup became one of the most successful restaurant booking apps in Hong Kong.

After experiencing the situation with Martin and Shyamala, it became apparent that there is a need for a comprehensive guide to organizational growth. As such, I have taken the initiative to compile information on this topic and create a guide to help businesses achieve growth.

In this book, I explore a variety of topics that are essential for fostering growth within organizations. Each chapter is dedicated to a specific topic, providing readers with a comprehensive explanation of its importance and how it can benefit an organization's growth.

To further illustrate the practical application of these topics, I analyze top companies in their respective industry and their approaches to implementing these concepts. By examining real-world case studies, readers understand how these strategies can be effectively implemented and adapted to their organization's unique needs.

In addition to analyzing case studies, I pose thought-provoking questions to readers, encouraging them to think critically about the decision-making process of the featured companies. These exercises help readers develop their analytical skills and think more strategically about their organization's growth.

To conclude each chapter, I provide actionable steps and practical tips that readers can use to implement these concepts within their organization. By delivering tangible strategies for implementation, readers are empowered to take concrete steps toward achieving growth and success in their organization.

The guide covers a broad range of topics, starting with branding and marketing. It is crucial to have a strong brand image and effective marketing strategies to attract and retain customers. Sales and customer relationships are also critical components, as they directly impact revenue and customer loyalty.

Employee training and development are equally important, as a skilled and motivated workforce can drive business success. Innovation and diversification are other areas that businesses need to focus on to remain competitive and adapt to changing market conditions.

Digital transformation is now more critical than ever, with the rise of technology and the increasing need for businesses to have a solid online presence. In addition, financial management is crucial, as proper financial planning and budgeting can help companies to make informed decisions and manage risks.

Partnerships and collaborations can provide significant growth opportunities through joint ventures or strategic alliances. Continuous improvement is another area that businesses need to focus on, as it helps them identify areas for improvement and implement solutions.

Training and development programs can also help businesses develop their employees' skills and capabilities, making them more effective and efficient. Data-driven decision-making is another essential aspect of organizational growth, as it allows companies to make informed decisions based on data and insights.

Sustainable business practices are becoming increasingly important as customers and investors are more conscious of environmental and social impacts. Global expansion is another area that businesses need to consider to tap into new markets and reach a broader customer base.

Lastly, mergers and acquisitions can provide significant opportunities for growth, whether it's through acquiring new technology, expanding into new markets, or diversifying the product portfolio.

The guide to organizational growth covers a broad range of topics that are critical to business success. By implementing the strategies and recommendations outlined in the guide, businesses can achieve sustained growth and remain competitive in today's dynamic business environment.

To immerse yourself in the content of "The Growth Matrix," consider finding a quiet, distraction-free space to focus on the material. Begin by reading the table of contents to get a sense of the topics covered, then dive into the introduction to better understand the author's perspective and goals for the book.

As you read each chapter, note critical points and insights that resonate with you, and consider how you can apply these ideas to your organization. Then, occasionally pause to reflect on what you've learned and consider how to implement the strategies presented in the book.

Engage with the material by asking yourself questions and considering how to adapt the ideas to suit your unique circumstances. By actively engaging with the content, you can understand the growth strategies presented in the book and apply them effectively to your organization.

> *- Rajalingam Rathinam*
> *raja@rajalingamrathinam.com*
> *rajalingamrathinam.com*
>
> *Bengaluru | Sydney*
> *April, 2023*

Introduction

This book, "The Growth Matrix," long explores various strategies organizations can implement to achieve growth. The strategies covered in the book include branding and marketing, sales, customer relationship management, employee training and development, innovation, diversification, digital transformation, financial management, partnerships, continuous improvement, data-driven decision-making, sustainable business practices, global expansion, and mergers and acquisitions.

The book draws on leading organizations' case studies to provide a practical understanding of these strategies. The aim is to examine how these organizations successfully implemented these strategies and to relate their experiences to the leadership teams of other organizations.

The book questions how these organizations achieved their growth and offer insights and lessons learned that can be applied to your organizations. By exploring these strategies, the book aims to help leaders understand the critical drivers of growth and identify the most effective method to achieve their organizational goals.

One of the key strategies discussed in the book is branding and marketing. The book examines how leading organizations have successfully built their brand and used marketing to create awareness and interest in their products or services. The book also looks at how sales strategies can drive growth through targeted sales campaigns, practical sales training, and implementing sales metrics to track performance.

Another strategy covered in the book is customer relationship management. The book examines how organizations can use customer data to understand customers better and build relationships that drive loyalty and growth. The book also explores employee training and development as a strategy for growth, looking at how organizations can develop their talent and create a learning culture to drive innovation and continuous improvement.

The book explores the role of innovation in driving growth, looking at how leading organizations have successfully implemented innovative strategies to create new products, services, and business models. The book also examines how organizations can use diversification to expand their reach and minimize risk and how digital transformation can optimize operations and create new growth opportunities.

The book explores the importance of financial management in achieving growth, examining strategies for managing cash flow, reducing costs, and investing in growth opportunities. The book also looks at the role of partnerships in driving growth, including the benefits of collaboration and strategic alliances.

Other strategies covered in the book include continuous improvement, data-driven decision-making, sustainable business practices, global expansion, and mergers and acquisitions. Throughout the book, case studies illustrate how leading organizations have successfully implemented these strategies and provide insights that can be applied to other organizations.

"The Growth Matrix" offers a comprehensive and practical guide to achieving growth in today's competitive business environment. Drawing on real-life case studies from leading organizations across the globe, the book provides valuable insights and actionable strategies that can be adapted to any organization seeking growth. From managing cash flow and reducing costs to investing in growth opportunities and forming strategic partnerships, the book covers a wide range of topics essential for driving growth. The author's expertise and deep understanding of the subject matter make this book an essential resource for anyone seeking to achieve sustainable growth and long-term success. Whether you are an entrepreneur, business owner, or executive, "The Growth Matrix" is a must-read book that can help you unlock the potential of your organization and drive growth..

The Growth Matrix

Organization Growth

"Organizational growth is not solely measured by the scale, but by the extent of its vision and impact. It requires cultivating resilience, embracing change, and empowering individuals to reach their full potential."

Organizational growth is expanding a business, improving its efficiency and effectiveness, and increasing its overall success. The importance of this growth cannot be overstated, as it significantly impacts the success and longevity of a business. In this, I will explain the importance of organizational change in terms of increased revenue, efficiency, competitiveness, reputation, and employee morale.

When a company grows, it can reach more customers, sell more products, and expand its product line. This leads to increased sales, higher profits, and more revenue. This increased revenue can then be reinvested into the business to continue its growth, creating a positive growth cycle and increased revenue.

With growth, the company can invest in new technologies, tools, and systems that improve its operations. This leads to a reduction in waste, an increase in productivity, and an overall improvement in the efficiency of the business. This improved efficiency results in lower costs and higher profits, further driving the company's growth.

With increased resources, a company can invest in new products, services, and marketing efforts to differentiate itself from competitors. This increased competitiveness can lead to a larger market share, increasing revenue and profitability. In addition, a growing company can also attract and retain the best employees, further enhancing its competitiveness.

Due to the increased visibility of the company, the recognition of its products and services, and the trust and confidence it builds with its customers. A strong reputation helps a company attract new customers, retain existing ones, and expand into new markets.

The employees feel a sense of pride and satisfaction in working for a thriving organization. This increased morale leads to higher engagement and productivity, which drives the company's growth. A growing company can offer its employees opportunities for career advancement, training and development, and job security, further enhancing employee morale.

Organizational growth is a critical aspect of any growing company. It increases revenue, efficiency, competitiveness, reputation, and employee morale. These benefits, in turn, drive the company's continued growth and contribute to its overall success. Therefore, companies must prioritize organizational growth and make investments that support this growth. This may include investing in new technologies, tools, and systems, expanding into new markets, and attracting and retaining the best employees. By doing so, companies can ensure their continued success and longevity in the marketplace.

Organizations implement many ways to improve and grow; many crucial strategies can help them achieve this.

From branding and marketing to employee engagement and culture, these strategies cover all aspects of an organization and can help drive growth, increase efficiency, and improve customer satisfaction.

Branding and Marketing

They are creating a solid brand image, developing marketing strategies to increase brand visibility and improve customer experience, and effectively communicating the brand message to the target audience. A strong brand helps organizations stand out, build customer loyalty, and increase revenue. In addition, effective marketing strategies can help organizations reach their target audience and drive sales.

Sales Growth

They identify new market opportunities, improve product offerings, and increase sales through effective strategies and tactics. By focusing on sales growth, organizations can increase revenue, reach new customers, and stay ahead of the competition.

Customer Satisfaction

Understanding customer needs, delivering high-quality products and services, and continuously improving the customer experience to increase loyalty and retain customers. Organizations can build strong customer relationships, increase customer loyalty, and drive repeat business by focusing on customer satisfaction.

Employee Engagement and Culture

It creates a positive and supportive work environment, providing opportunities for professional development and growth and promoting a culture of collaboration and teamwork. By fostering a positive and supportive workplace culture, organizations can improve employee satisfaction, increase retention, and enhance performance.

Innovation

It encourages and fosters a culture of innovation, invests in research and development, and continuously improves products, services, and processes to stay ahead of the competition. By embracing innovation, organizations can differentiate themselves, increase efficiency, and drive growth.

Diversification

They are expanding the product or service offering into new markets, entering new industries, and exploring new business opportunities to mitigate risk and increase revenue. By diversifying their operations, organizations can reduce dependence on a single product or market, increase revenue, and improve their competitiveness.

Digital Transformation

Leveraging technology to improve operations, increase efficiency, and enhance customer experiences. Organizations can improve processes, increase productivity, and enhance the customer experience by adopting digital solutions.

Financial Management

How we manage cash flow, reduce costs, and maximize profits through sound financial planning and management. As a result, organizations can ensure financial stability, reduce risk, and increase profits by implementing good financial management practices.

Collaboration and Partnerships

Forming strategic partnerships and collaborations with other organizations to increase market reach, access new resources, and increase competitive advantage. By collaborating with other organizations, companies can access new markets, customers, and resources and improve their competitiveness.

Continuous Improvement

This involves continuously analyzing and improving processes, products, and services to increase efficiency, reduce waste, and enhance the customer experience. This can include implementing best practices and utilizing data and analytics to identify areas for improvement. As a result, organizations can stay ahead of the competition by continuously improving and ensuring long-term success.

Employee Training and Development

Investing in employees' professional development through training programs, mentorship, and educational opportunities to increase skill sets and improve job performance. Organizations can increase employee satisfaction, retention, and overall performance by providing employees with opportunities to learn and grow.

Data-Driven Decision Making

Using data and analytics to inform decision-making, measure performance, and identify areas for improvement. Organizations can make informed, evidence-based decisions that drive growth and success by leveraging data and analytics.

Sustainable Business Practices

Adopting environmentally and socially responsible business practices to reduce waste, minimize environmental harm, and enhance the organization's reputation. By operating sustainably, organizations can build a positive reputation, attract customers and employees who share their values, and ensure long-term success.

Global Expansion

Expanding operations into international markets to increase market reach, access new customers, and reduce dependence on domestic markets. By expanding globally, organizations can tap into new markets, increase revenue, and improve their competitive position.

Mergers and Acquisitions

Acquiring or merging with other companies to increase market share, access new resources, and increase competitive advantage. Companies can access new markets, customers, and resources by accepting or connecting with other organizations and improving their competitiveness.

Each of these strategies can play a crucial role in driving organizational growth and success. It's essential for organizations to consider the unique needs of their business and to choose strategies that align with their goals and objectives.

In today's competitive environment, from improving branding and marketing to embracing digital transformation, numerous strategies can help organizations reach their goals and drive success. Organizations must consider their unique needs and choose strategies aligning with their goals and objectives. By implementing effective organizational growth strategies, companies can increase efficiency, improve customer satisfaction, and ultimately drive long-term success.

The Growth Matrix

Branding & Marketing for Growth

> *"Branding and marketing can fuel growth by improving brand recognition, loyalty, sales, morale, confidence, differentiation, and reputation."*

    I used to embark on a morning walk from Sector 2 of the HSR Layout in Bengaluru, traversing the Outer Ring Road to reach Agara and then back to BDA Complex to savor the freshly brewed South Indian coffee at a local coffee shop. While this establishment had been in operation for a few years, I observed a concerning trend wherein new patrons were scarce, and even regular customers had begun to abandon it. As an astute observer, I ascertained that the absence of a strong brand image and effective marketing strategy thwarted its growth.

    I conversed with the proprietor, who hailed from a small village near Bengaluru, to make him cognizant of the pressing need to focus on branding and marketing. I assisted him in creating a logo, tagline, color scheme, and style, besides steering him to invest in social media advertising and promotional activities, all aimed at augmenting brand awareness and targeting local coffee connoisseurs through captivating visuals and messaging. I also enlisted the support of my acquaintances to collaborate with neighboring businesses to host events and promotions that would entice a wider audience.

Moreover, I emphasized the importance of delivering excellent products and services to foster customer loyalty while establishing a unique brand identity that would stand out in the marketplace. I devoted considerable time to training the staff to provide exemplary customer service and ensure that the coffee shop offered a welcoming and cozy ambiance that would delight the customers.

To generate a buzz around the establishment, I introduced a rotation of different flavors each day of the week, circulated a flavor calendar, and initiated engagement activities on social media and at the store level. I also imbued the theme of 'Happiness' in the coffee shop, creating an upbeat and cheerful environment that would engender smiles on customers' faces.

My concerted efforts bore fruit as the coffee shop began to differentiate itself from its competitors, attracting a growing clientele and increasing sales. The owner was also able to command premium prices for his coffee and other products, as customers recognized the high-quality and distinctive nature of the brand. Subsequently, I acquainted him with a franchise model, enabling him to expand his business to encompass 45 outlets across Bengaluru.

The positive reputation and brand image of the coffee shop also had a ripple effect on employee morale and engagement. The staff felt a sense of pride and accomplishment in working for a flourishing and expanding establishment, which motivated them to provide even better customer service and contribute to the brand's continued success.

Branding and marketing play a crucial role in the growth of an organization by building and maintaining a strong image and reputation in the market. Here are a few ways branding and marketing can help an organization grow.

Increased Awareness

Effective branding and marketing strategies help organizations increase brand awareness and reach a wider audience. This can be achieved through various means, such as advertising, social media, public relations, and events. By getting a wider audience, organizations can introduce their products or services to a larger group of potential customers and increase their chances of attracting new business.

Customer Loyalty

A strong brand image and reputation can lead to customer loyalty, as customers are likelier to choose a brand they trust and have a positive idea of. In addition, a consistent brand message and high-quality products or services can help build customer trust and loyalty, leading to repeat business and positive word-of-mouth referrals.

Differentiation

Effective branding and marketing strategies can help organizations differentiate themselves from their competitors, making it easier for customers to identify and choose their products or services. By establishing a unique brand image and positioning in the market, organizations can stand out and be remembered by customers, increasing the likelihood of being chosen over competitors.

Increased Sales

Organizations can increase their sales and revenue by building a solid brand image and reputation. A well-established brand can command a higher price for its products and services, as customers are willing to pay more for a product or service from a trusted and reputable brand. In addition, a strong brand can also drive new business and increase the frequency of purchases from existing customers.

Employee Engagement

A strong brand image can also help organizations attract and retain employees, as employees are more likely to be proud to work for an organization with a positive image and reputation. A strong brand can also help increase employee morale and motivation, leading to improved performance and a more engaged workforce.

Investor Confidence

A strong brand image and reputation can also increase investor confidence, as investors are more likely to invest in an organization with a strong brand and positive impression. In addition, investors are often more likely to invest in an organization with a clear and consistent brand message, high-quality products or services, and a positive reputation in the market.

Reputation Management

Effective branding and marketing strategies can help organizations manage their online and offline reputations. This can involve monitoring and responding to customer feedback, managing negative publicity, and proactively promoting positive brand messages and stories. By managing their reputation, organizations can maintain a positive image in the market and protect their brand from harm.

Illustrating through practical examples

This American multinational conglomerate with a long history in the healthcare industry is one of the world's largest producers of consumer healthcare products and operates in numerous countries and markets. All their's brand is synonymous with quality, reliability, and trust, and the company has used branding and marketing strategies to maintain and grow its position in the healthcare market.

It has a strong presence in the healthcare industry, with a wide range of products and services that cater to the needs of consumers and healthcare professionals. The company has leveraged various marketing channels, including traditional media, digital media, and events, to reach its target audience and increase brand awareness. For example, the company has invested heavily in television advertising to promote its over-the-counter (OTC) products, such as Paracetamol and adhesive bandage. The company has also established a solid online presence through its website, social media channels, and mobile apps, which provide consumers with information about its products and services. It has sponsored several healthcare events and conferences, allowing the company to engage with its target audience and raise awareness about its brand.

The multinational has built a strong reputation for quality and reliability, which has helped the company establish a loyal customer base. The company's brand is well-known for producing high-quality consumer healthcare products that customers can trust. The company's reputation for quality has helped it command a premium price for its derivatives, as customers are willing to pay more for a product from a trusted brand. The company has also built loyalty through its customer service and support, which is widely regarded as some of the best in the industry. Through these efforts, the company has retained its customers and generated repeat business, which has helped the company grow its market share.

This healthcare conglomerate has differentiated itself from its competitors in the healthcare industry by offering a wide range of products and services that cater to the needs of consumers and healthcare professionals. The company has established a unique brand image and positioning in the market, which has helped it to stand out and be remembered by customers. The company has also differentiated itself in the pharmaceuticals market by investing in research and development and introducing innovative products, such as cancer treatments.

It's brand value has helped to drive sales and revenue. The company's commitment to providing high-quality products and services has resulted in a loyal customer base willing to pay a premium for its products. It's focus on innovation has also driven sales by introducing new and innovative products to the market, such as cancer treatments and medical devices. Additionally, the company's customer loyalty program 'Care Club' has helped to drive repeat business, further contributing to its sales growth.

It's strong brand image and reputation have helped to attract and retain employees, as employees are proud to work for a company with a positive image and reputation. The company's focus on employee engagement has also helped to increase employee morale and motivation, leading to improved performance and a more engaged workforce. In addition, the company provides its employees with opportunities for professional development, such as training and education programs. Finally, it encourages them to participate in the company's initiatives and initiatives actively.

The brand reputation has also increased investor confidence, as investors are more likely to invest in a company with a strong brand and positive image. The company's commitment to providing high-quality products and services and its focus on innovation have helped build a positive market reputation and increase investor confidence. In addition, it's strong financial performance and solid track record have further boosted investor confidence.

It has a robust reputation management strategy to manage its online and offline reputation. The brand's reputation management strategy focuses on proactively communicating with its stakeholders and being transparent about potential risks or concerns. The company has a crisis management plan and has effectively responded to negative publicity to minimize its impact on the brand. In addition, it uses social media and other digital channels to monitor and manage its online reputation, ensuring its brand image remains favorable and trustworthy.

Take your time and try to answer these questions.

1) How does it's brand positioning in the healthcare market set it apart from its competitors, and what can your organization learn from this approach?

2) Can you discuss how it leverages customer loyalty to drive repeat business and positive word-of-mouth referrals and how this can be replicated in your organization?

3) How does it's commitment to employee engagement and motivation contribute to its overall success, and what steps can your organization take to foster a similar environment?

4) Can you discuss the role of crisis management and response strategies in protecting a brand's reputation and what lessons your organization can learn from It's approach?

5) How does they measure the success of its branding and marketing efforts, and what metrics and KPIs should your organization track to evaluate the impact of its branding and marketing strategies?

How can it work for you?

Understanding the value and impact of branding and marketing on organizational growth and success is essential. By analyzing their case study, you can identify key strategies and best practices that can be adapted and applied to your organization. For example, you can evaluate the potential of leveraging customer loyalty to drive repeat business, the importance of consistent brand messaging, the role of employee engagement in promoting a positive brand image, and the need for effective crisis management and reputation management strategies.

By taking a strategic and proactive approach to branding and marketing, you can increase your organization's brand awareness, differentiate yourself from competitors, build customer loyalty, and foster a positive reputation in the market. This, in turn, can drive growth, improve revenue, and increase investor confidence in your organization.

It is essential to regularly assess and evaluate the impact of your branding and marketing strategies and to make adjustments and optimizations as needed. Utilizing metrics and KPIs can help you understand the effectiveness of your efforts and make informed decisions to improve your approach continuously.

In today's highly competitive business landscape, it's more important than ever for organizations to effectively leverage branding and marketing strategies to stand out and drive growth. However, simply implementing a strategy is not enough. Regularly assessing and evaluating the impact of your efforts is essential to understand their effectiveness and make necessary adjustments.

The readers can use the below table to assess their organization's current status and set goals, action plans, and timelines for improving each aspect of branding and marketing. In addition, the positive and negative columns can be used to anticipate potential outcomes and prepare for any challenges.

The Growth Matrix

Key Aspect	Current Status	Positive Aspects	Negative Aspects	Goals	Action Plan	Timeline
Increased brand awareness						
Customer loyalty						
Differentiation						
Increased Sales						
Employee Engagement						
Investor Confidence						
Reputation Management						

Your organization's success depends on your ability to continuously assess and optimize your branding and marketing strategies. By setting measurable goals, tracking relevant metrics, and anticipating potential outcomes, you can make informed decisions that drive growth and create a meaningful impact. Let us help guide you on this journey, providing expert insights and resources to ensure your continued success.

To learn more about how your organization can leverage the power of branding and marketing to drive growth and success, we would be pleased to offer their insight and expertise. We would love to hear from you on your journey toward development and would be happy to provide any additional support and resources you may need along the way.

Sales for Growth

> *"Sales growth is key to success. Expand revenue and market reach by tapping into new markets, improving products, using effective sales strategies, and staying ahead of the competition."*

During our monthly meeting, the founders of a consulting startup based in the Philippines shared concerns about the sales performance of their new product, a cloud-based project management software (PMS). Despite its innovative features, such as real-time collaboration, automated workflows, and analytics dashboard, the sales figures needed to meet their expectations.

As a consultant, I suggested developing a comprehensive sales growth strategy to increase revenue, reach new customers, and stay ahead of the competition. We began by identifying new market opportunities in the Philippines, such as small and medium-sized enterprises (SMEs) that needed a cost-effective and easy-to-use project management solution.

We conducted extensive market research to understand the target audience and the current market landscape. We analyzed consumer behavior and demographics, monitored industry and market trends, and identified a gap in the market that PMS could fill.

Next, we focused on improving the product offering by investing in research and development to enhance its features and functionality. We incorporated customer feedback and insights into the product design to ensure that PMS provided the best solution to meet customers' needs. As a result, we added features such as Gantt charts, time tracking, and resource allocation to make PMS more versatile and user-friendly.

To build a strong brand identity, we created marketing materials that effectively communicated the message of PMS's benefits and unique value proposition. As a result, we consistently delivered high-quality products and services and formulated a strong sales pipeline tracking leads, opportunities, and deals. We prioritized the sales efforts to maximize the chances of closing deals. We worked on building a customer-focused culture, providing excellent customer service, and building strategic partnerships with other businesses and organizations to cross-promote the product.

We leveraged digital channels such as social media, email marketing, and e-commerce platforms to build the PMS brand, engage with potential customers, and drive sales cost-effectively and efficiently. We also organized a workshop for the leadership team to educate them on the importance of a customer-centric approach and how to align their sales efforts with the customers' needs.

As a result of the sales growth strategy, PMS's revenue began to increase. Within six months, we secured contracts with over 50 SMEs in the Philippines, resulting in a 35% increase in revenue. We also expanded our market share, reaching new customers in Southeast Asian countries such as Indonesia and Thailand.

As a crucial part of our sales growth strategy, we recognized the importance of identifying potential implementation and technical partners to expand our reach in the market further. Therefore, we assembled a dedicated team of B2B marketers to identify potential partners across Southeast Asia and the Middle East. This team conducted extensive research and analysis to identify suitable partners, focusing on those with complementary product offerings and a strong reputation in their respective markets.

The efforts of our B2B marketing team proved to be fruitful, as we were able to establish partnerships with several implementation and technical partners across the region. These partnerships enabled us to tap into new markets, reach new customers, and expand our sales channels. As a result, our sales revenue grew by an impressive 31% the following year.

The partnerships we established were built on mutual trust and understanding, allowing us to work closely with our partners to develop customized solutions for our customers. Through our combined expertise and resources, we were able to deliver innovative products and services that met the needs of our customers while also driving growth for our respective businesses.

Our success in establishing these partnerships can be attributed to our diligent approach to research and analysis and our commitment to delivering value to our partners and customers. Moving forward, we will continue to build strategic partnerships and collaborations that will help us expand our reach and drive sales growth while delivering exceptional value to our customers.

The founders were pleased with the results and acknowledged the importance of a well-crafted sales growth strategy. We continued to monitor our sales metrics, analyze data, and adjust our strategy and tactics accordingly. PMS became a well-established brand in the industry, with a growing customer base and a reputation for delivering innovative project management solutions. We remained committed to our sales growth strategy, continuously identifying new market opportunities, improving our product offering, and executing effective sales strategies and tactics to stay ahead of the competition—the crucial topic of sales growth and how it drives revenue, market reach, and competitiveness. We aim to help you understand the importance of identifying new market opportunities, improving product offerings, and executing effective sales strategies and tactics.

Sales growth is crucial to organizational change, impacting revenue and market reach. Companies looking to grow and succeed in today's competitive business environment must identify new market opportunities, improve their product offerings, and execute sales strategies and tactics effectively.

To identify new market opportunities, companies must first conduct market research to understand their target audience and the current market landscape. This can involve analyzing consumer behavior and demographics and monitoring industry and market trends. Based on the insights gained from this research, companies can determine the areas where they can fill a gap in the market. Then, companies can tap into new market opportunities and increase their customer base by developing products or services to meet these unmet needs.

Companies must focus on improving their product offerings. This can involve investing in research and development to create new products or services or enhance existing ones. Companies can also improve their product offerings by incorporating customer feedback and insights into their product design, ensuring that they are providing the best possible solutions to meet the needs of their customers.

Once new market opportunities have been identified, and product offerings have been improved, companies must focus on sales strategies and tactics. Effective sales strategies and tactics can help companies reach new customers, increase their market share, and stay ahead of the competition. Some common strategies and tactics include:

Developing a Strong Brand

Companies with strong brands are more likely to be recognized by consumers and are better positioned to win new customers. This involves developing a clear brand identity, creating marketing materials that effectively communicate the brand's message, and consistently delivering high-quality products and services.

Building a Sales Pipeline

Effective Sales pipeline strategy helps organizations track leads, opportunities, and deals and prioritize their sales efforts to maximize their chances of closing deals. A well-designed sales pipeline should be able to effectively manage the sales process from start to finish, ensuring that sales teams have the information and resources they need to succeed. Organizations can drive sustainable sales growth and achieve tremendous success in today's competitive business environment by investing in developing and maintaining a strong sales pipeline.

Leveraging Digital Channels

Digital channels such as social media, email marketing, and e-commerce platforms allow companies to build their brand, engage with potential customers, and drive sales cost-effectively and efficiently. By creating a solid online presence, companies can reach a wider audience and expand their reach beyond traditional marketing methods. Additionally, digital channels allow companies to collect valuable customer data and insights, which can be used to improve their sales strategies and tactics further. Organizations must clearly understand their target audience to effectively leverage digital channels and develop a strategic approach that aligns with their overall sales and marketing goals.

Providing Excellent Customer Service

Companies that provide excellent customer service are likelier to win repeat business and build customer loyalty. This involves creating a customer-focused culture, investing in training and development for customer service staff, and consistently delivering high-quality service.

Building Strategic Partnerships

Companies can increase sales by building strategic partnerships with other businesses, organizations, and influencers. Companies can cross-promote their products and services, reach new customers, and drive sales by working together.

The sales growth and its impact on organizational development provided valuable insights and actionable tips to help you drive revenue, reach new customers, and stay ahead of the competition.

Illustrating through practical examples

A real-life example of a company that has successfully followed these steps is a leading British multinational consumer goods company in the fast-moving consumer goods (FMCG) industry. To name a few, this FMCG is known for its iconic tea, soup, and soap brands. In addition, the company has a long-standing reputation for its commitment to sustainability, social responsibility, and its relentless focus on growth and innovation.

To identify new market opportunities, they conducted extensive market research to understand its target audience and the current market landscape. In addition, the company analyzed consumer behavior and demographics and monitored industry trends and market trends. Based on these insights, they identified a gap in the market for eco-friendly and sustainable products. To tap into this market opportunity, they launched its "Sustainable Living Plan," which aimed to reduce the environmental impact of its products and operations while improving millions of people's lives.

In addition to identifying new market opportunities, it also focused on improving its product offerings. The company invested heavily in research and development to create and enhance new products. For example, this FMCG company launched a range of eco-friendly and sustainable household cleaning products under a 'ECO' specific brand. The products are made from natural, plant-based ingredients and are packaged in recyclable materials.

Once new market opportunities had been identified and product offerings improved, they turned their attention to sales strategies and tactics. The company developed a strong brand by creating a clear brand identity, creating marketing materials that effectively communicated its brand message, and consistently delivering high-quality products and services. To build its sales pipeline, it invested in technology to track leads, opportunities, and deals effectively.

This FMCG company also leveraged digital channels such as social media, email marketing, and e-commerce platforms to reach new customers and increase sales. The company built its brand by engaging with potential customers through these channels, and by using them effectively, It was able to drive sales.

To provide excellent customer service, this FMCG company created a customer-focused culture, invested in training and development for customer service staff, and consistently delivered high-quality service. This helped the company win repeat business and build customer loyalty.

To increase sales, it built strategic partnerships with other businesses, organizations, and influencers. By working together, the company could cross-promote its products and services, reach new customers, and drive sales.

The success of this company in the FMCG industry is a prime example of how focusing on sales growth through effective sales strategies and tactics can drive revenue, market reach, and competitiveness. The company's relentless focus on identifying new market opportunities, improving its product offerings, and executing effective sales strategies and tactics has helped it remain a market leader and set the standard for other companies in the industry.

Take your time and try to answer these questions.

1) Can you describe the key strategies and tactics that the company used to drive sales growth and increase its market reach?

2) How did their investment in research and development help improve its product offerings and tap into new market opportunities?

3) Can you explain how this FMCG company's brand-building efforts helped them to win new customers and increase sales?

4) How did they leverage digital channels to reach new customers and drive sales?

5) Can you discuss the role of customer service in it's sales growth strategy and how it worked to build customer loyalty?

6) Can you describe how it made strategic partnerships to increase sales and reach new customers?

7) How did this FMCG company prioritize its sales efforts and track leads, opportunities, and deals through its sales pipeline?

8) What made this FMCG company's sales growth strategy successful, and how can other organizations apply similar principles?

9) Can you discuss the role of market research in it's sales growth strategy and how it helped them to identify new market opportunities?

10) What are the most critical takeaways from it's case study for organizations looking to drive sales growth and improve their market reach?

How can it work for you?

This case study provides a comprehensive guide for organizations looking to drive sales growth and improve their market reach. By taking a closer look at the key elements of their successful sales growth strategy, organizations can identify specific strategies and tactics they can implement in their businesses to achieve similar results.

One of the essential takeaways from the case study is identifying new market opportunities. Market research is crucial, as it helps organizations understand their target audience and the current market landscape. By analyzing consumer behavior and demographics and monitoring industry and market trends, organizations can determine areas in which they can fill a gap in the market. Organizations can tap into new market opportunities and increase their customer base by developing products or services to meet these unmet needs.

Improving product offerings is another critical aspect of driving sales growth, as it helps organizations stay ahead of the competition and meet the changing needs of their customers. Organizations can invest in research and development to create new products or services or enhance existing ones. In addition, incorporating customer feedback and insights into product design can help organizations improve their product offerings and provide the best solutions to meet their customers' needs.

Once new market opportunities have been identified and product offerings have been improved, organizations must focus on sales strategies and tactics. This case study highlights several practical strategies and tactics, including building a solid brand, leveraging digital channels, providing excellent customer service, and building strategic partnerships.

A strong brand is essential for organizations looking to be recognized by consumers and win new customers. This involves developing a clear brand identity, creating marketing materials that effectively communicate the brand's message, and consistently delivering high-quality products and services. In addition, leveraging digital channels, such as social media, email marketing, and e-commerce platforms, can help organizations reach new customers and increase sales.

Providing excellent customer service is another critical component of driving sales growth, as it helps organizations win repeat business and build customer loyalty. This involves creating a customer-focused culture, investing in training and development for customer service staff, and consistently delivering high-quality service. Finally, building strategic partnerships with other businesses, organizations, and influencers can help organizations cross-promote their products and services, reach new customers, and drive sales.

It is essential for organizations to evaluate and refine their sales strategies and tactics regularly and to strive for improvement and innovation continuously. By under-standing the key elements of it's successful sales growth strategy, organizations can develop their customized approach to driving sales growth and improving their market reach.

Boosting Organizational Growth Through Effective Sales Strategies and Tactics has provided valuable insights and actionable tips for your organization to drive revenue, reach new customers, and stay ahead of the competition. We encourage you to take the next step and evaluate your organization's strengths, weaknesses, and opportunities for growth using the workable table in this article.

Key Aspects	Strengths	Weakness	Measurements	Actionable Steps
New Market				
Product Improvement				
Developing a Strong Brand				
Sales Pipeline				
Leveraging Digital				
Customer Service				
Strategic Partnership				

This table provides a framework for evaluating an organization's strengths and weaknesses and taking action to address areas for improvement. Organizations can drive growth and competitiveness by regularly assessing performance and taking action to improve.

By taking a measured and actionable approach, your organization can make informed decisions that will lead to sustainable sales growth and drive overall organizational success. We would love to hear from you on your journey toward development and would be happy to provide any additional support and resources you may need along the way.

The Growth Matrix

Building Customer Relationships for Growth

"Customer satisfaction is the key to unlocking growth and success for organizations. It begins with a deep understanding of customer needs and a relentless commitment to delivering a superior experience."

In September 2018, I was conducting a seminar for a small group of invitees on customer satisfaction in a startup Hub in Sydney; I met Mr. Michael Scott, who was heading a biotech company in Melbourne. The company faced a significant challenge with customer satisfaction, and they needed more focus on their needs to retain customers. In addition, they had noticed a decline in their customer base and were worried about its impact on their growth and success.

Upon my arrival, I conducted an initial assessment of the company's operations and customer feedback data. The feedback data showed that customers wanted a better quality of the company's products and services. In addition, many reported needing more time to receive their orders and better customer service when trying to follow up on their orders.

After analyzing the data, I shared my findings with the company's leadership team. We discussed the importance of understanding customer needs and how this could be achieved by gathering feedback via surveys and other channels. We also discussed the need for a data-driven approach to decision-making and the importance of investing in quality control measures and employee training programs to ensure that the company's products and services met customer needs.

The company's leadership team was receptive to these ideas, and we worked together to develop a plan to improve customer satisfaction. We implemented a new customer feedback system that allowed us to gather feedback in real-time and respond to customer needs quickly. We also invested in employee training programs to improve customer service and product quality.

Over the next few months, we saw a significant improvement in customer satisfaction. Customers were happy with the quality of the company's products and services, and they reported experiencing fewer delays in receiving their orders. As a result, the company's reputation improved, and we saw an increase in repeat business.

The leadership team was thrilled with the results and recognized the importance of continuing to focus on customer satisfaction to drive growth and success. They committed to ongoing customer feedback and continuous improvement initiatives to remain competitive.

As I concluded my coaching engagement with the company, I felt proud of our progress. It was satisfying to see how a data-driven approach to customer satisfaction could impact a business. By focusing on understanding customer needs, delivering high-quality products and services, and continuously improving the customer experience, the company has transformed its reputation and laid the groundwork for future growth and success.The importance of understanding customer needs, delivering high-quality products and services, and continuously improving the customer experience to drive growth and success for organizations.

Customer satisfaction is a crucial aspect of any organization's growth strategy. A satisfied customer is more likely to become loyal, which leads to increased repeat business and helps build a strong reputation for the company. In today's competitive business landscape, companies must understand the needs of their customers and deliver high-quality products and services that meet and exceed those needs. This requires a focus on continuous improvement and a commitment to providing a superior customer experience.

Studies have shown that a satisfied customer is more likely to remain a customer for longer. In fact, according to a study by the Harvard Business Review, companies that increase customer satisfaction by just 5% can see a corresponding increase in customer loyalty of up to 25%. This highlights the importance of customer satisfaction in retaining customers and driving repeat business.

To achieve customer satisfaction, companies must take a data-driven approach to understand the needs of their customers. This includes gathering feedback through various channels such as surveys, social media, and customer service interactions. This feedback can be analyzed to identify areas where the company can improve its products, services, and customer experience.

For example, suppose many customers complain about long wait times when trying to reach customer service. In that case, the company can invest in hiring more customer service representatives or improving its call center technology to reduce wait times. As a result, the company can improve the overall customer experience and increase customer satisfaction by addressing these issues.

The critical aspect of customer satisfaction is providing high-quality products and services. Companies must ensure that their products meet customer needs, perform as expected, and deliver services promptly and efficiently. Companies must invest in quality control measures, employee training programs, and continuous improvement initiatives to achieve this.

Most companies use customer user surveys to improve product recommendations, delivery times, and product quality. By understanding customer needs, delivering high-quality products and services, and continuously improving the customer experience, companies can build strong relationships, increase customer loyalty, and drive repeat business. In addition, by taking a data-driven approach to customer satisfaction, companies can make informed decisions that help them achieve their growth objectives and remain competitive in today's business landscape.

Illustrating through practical examples

This leading Spanish clothing and accessories retailer that has experienced tremendous growth and success by focusing on customer satisfaction. As a result, the company has stayed ahead of the competition by understanding its customers' needs and continuously improving the customer experience.

In this case study, we will explore how It has achieved customer satisfaction and has driven growth and success for the company.

Understanding Customer Needs

It has understood customers' needs by collecting and analyzing data from various sources. The company has implemented a sophisticated data analytics system to track customer behavior and preferences. This data is used to inform product design and development, ensuring that it's offerings meet the needs and wants of its customers.

For example, suppose it's data analytics system reveals that customers are looking for more environmentally-friendly clothing options. In that case, the company can respond by introducing a line of clothing made from sustainable materials. By staying in tune with its customers' needs and wants, it can maintain its relevance in the market and continue to grow.

Delivering High-Quality Products and Services

It has a reputation for delivering high-quality products and services. The company has a strict quality control process, including regular checks and audits of its products and services. This helps to ensure that its products meet the expectations of its customers and perform as expected.

In addition, it has invested in training programs for its employees to help them provide the best possible customer service. This investment has paid off, as the company's employees are knowledgeable and professional, providing a positive experience for customers. This, in turn, has helped to build trust and loyalty with It's customers.

Continuously Improving the Customer Experience

It is committed to continuously improving the customer experience. The company uses customer feedback to identify areas for improvement and implements changes to enhance the customer experience. For example, suppose customers complain about long wait times when trying to reach customer service. In that case, it can invest in hiring more customer service representatives or improving its call center technology to reduce wait times.

It has implemented an omnichannel approach to retailing, making it easier for customers to shop with the company through multiple channels, such as online, in-store, and mobile devices. This has helped to improve the customer experience, as customers can choose the medium that best suits their needs.

Impact on Growth and Success

Their focus on customer satisfaction has significantly impacted its growth and success. The company's reputation for delivering high-quality products and services and its commitment to continuously improving the customer experience have helped build strong relationships with its customers.

As a result, it has experienced increased repeat business, as satisfied customers are likelier to become loyal customers. This, in turn, has helped to drive the company's growth and success. In addition, it's data-driven approach to customer satisfaction has enabled it to make informed decisions that have helped it achieve its growth objectives and remain competitive in the retail industry.

This Spanish brand is a prime example of how a focus on customer satisfaction can drive growth and success for an organization. By understanding its customers' needs, delivering high-quality products and services, and continuously improving the customer experience, This Spanish brand has built strong relationships with its customers and increased customer loyalty.

This highlights the importance of a data-driven approach to customer satisfaction, enabling companies to make informed decisions that help them achieve their growth objectives and remain competitive.

Take your time and try to answer these questions.

1) How does it prioritize customer satisfaction in its overall business strategy?

2) How does it gather and analyze customer feedback to inform its product offerings and customer experience?

3) Can you discuss it's approach to continuously improving the customer experience, and what steps does the company take to achieve this goal?

4) How does their focus on customer satisfaction drive growth and success for the company?

5) Can you discuss how it leverages data and technology to understand customer needs and improve the customer experience?

6) How does their commitment to customer satisfaction help the company maintain a competitive advantage in the fashion retail industry?

7) Can you discuss the impact of their focus on customer satisfaction on customer loyalty and repeat business?

8) How does it balance the need to deliver high-quality products and services with the need to remain cost-effective and profitable?

9) How does it ensure its employees align with its focus on customer satisfaction, and what role do they play in driving this effort?

10) What lessons can other organizations learn from It's approach to customer satisfaction, and what steps can they take to implement similar strategies in their businesses?

How can it work for you?

Integrating this Spanish brand's approach into one's organization requires careful analysis and consideration of the specific business challenges and opportunities. By reflecting on the key strategies and practices that have driven it's success in customer satisfaction, organizations can identify opportunities to apply similar approaches to their operations. This can involve assessing the current state of customer satisfaction, gathering and analyzing customer feedback, identifying areas for improvement, and implementing changes to the customer experience.

To start, leaders should assess customer satisfaction and identify improvement areas. This can involve gathering customer feedback through surveys, social media, and customer service interactions and analyzing this feedback to identify trends and areas for improvement. Organizations can make informed decisions about improving the customer experience by taking a data-driven approach to customer satisfaction.

Once areas for improvement have been identified, organizations should focus on implementing changes that will drive customer satisfaction. This can involve investing in new technology, improving product quality, and enhancing the customer experience through better employee training and support. Organizations should also consider how they can continuously improve the customer experience through regular customer feedback, continuous improvement initiatives, and a focus on innovation.

To ensure that customer satisfaction remains a top priority, organizations should involve all employees to drive customer satisfaction. This can include creating a customer-centric culture, providing employee training and support, and regularly communicating the importance of customer satisfaction. By aligning all employees around a common goal of delivering a superior customer experience, organizations can ensure that customer satisfaction remains a top priority and drives long-term growth and success.

The organizations should reflect on the lessons from the Spanish retailers case study and identify how they can apply them to their operations. This can involve a data-driven approach to customer satisfaction, investing in continuous improvement initiatives, and creating a customer-centric culture. By using these fundamental principles, organizations can achieve the same level of success as this Spanish brand in delivering customer satisfaction and driving growth and success for the business.

Understanding customer needs, delivering high-quality products and services, and continuously improving the customer experience cannot be overstated. By taking a data-driven approach to customer satisfaction, organizations can make informed decisions that help them achieve their growth objectives and remain competitive in today's business landscape.

Elements to Evaluate	Strengths	Weakness	Measurements	Actionable Steps
Understanding customer needs				
Delivery of high quality products and services				
Continuously improving the customer				

We encourage all organizations to take the time to assess their current customer satisfaction approach and identify improvement areas. Organizations can better understand their strengths and weaknesses using the self-assessment table provided and develop a measurable and actionable strategy to drive customer satisfaction and growth.

Let's work together to deliver exceptional customer experiences and drive business success.

Nurturing Employee Well-Being for Growth

"A positive workplace culture prioritizes growth, collaboration, and well-being can attract and retain top talent, boost performance, and drive long-term success."

Upon entering the fireworks manufacturing company in Sivakasi, Tamilnadu, India, I was immediately struck by the engaged and collaborative atmosphere among the employees. This small town produces 70% of India's firecrackers and matchsticks and 30% of the country's diaries. With a workforce of over 25,000, the estimated turnover of the town's industries is around ₹20 billion (US$250 million).

One of the company's directors, Mr. Sunder, affectionately called 'Annachi' by the employees, recognizes the importance of employee well-being and engagement and has implemented several practices to cultivate a positive and supportive work environment. For instance, the management encourages employees to engage in wellness activities like yoga and meditation to reduce stress levels and promote mental health. The organization also prioritizes employee development and growth by providing training and development opportunities to help employees advance in their careers. Additionally, the company promotes collaboration and teamwork, creating an inclusive work environment where all employees are treated with respect and dignity regardless of their position.

Implementing these practices has resulted in motivated and engaged employees who take pride in their contributions and provide high-quality products and services. This, in turn, has enhanced customer satisfaction and loyalty and improved the company's financial performance. Employees are more productive, take fewer sick days, and are less likely to leave the organization, resulting in lower turnover costs and reduced recruitment and training expenses.

Furthermore, the company's management goes above and beyond to care for their employees. They provide free education to the children of their laborers, particularly girls, until graduation. This underscores the organization's commitment to fostering a positive and supportive workplace culture.

The fireworks manufacturing company in Sivakasi is an excellent example of the benefits of investing in employee well-being and engagement. By prioritizing a positive and supportive workplace culture, organizations can enhance employee satisfaction, improve performance, and contribute to their overall success.Employee well-being and engagement. It's no secret that a happy and motivated workforce is critical to success, but how do you create a supportive and engaging work environment? The benefits of investing in employee well-being and engagement and exploring some of the best practices for creating a positive and productive workplace culture.

Employee engagement and culture play a crucial role in the success and growth of an organization. A positive and supportive work environment can significantly impact employee satisfaction, motivation, and overall performance.

A happy workplace culture helps to attract and retain top talent. When employees feel valued, respected, and supported; they are likelier to remain with the organization and contribute to its success. Additionally, a strong culture emphasizing employee development and growth can give employees the skills and opportunities to advance their careers, making the organization attractive.

When employees feel valued, they are more likely to be engaged in their work, take pride in their contributions, and feel invested in the organization's success. This leads to higher levels of job satisfaction, which has been shown to positively impact employee productivity and performance.

A positive workplace culture also supports collaboration and teamwork. Employees who feel supported and encouraged to work together are more likely to develop strong working relationships and collaborate effectively to achieve common goals. This can lead to higher levels of productivity and improved problem-solving and decision-making capabilities.

Moreover, a strong workplace culture can also positively impact employee health and well-being. A supportive work environment that prioritizes employee well-being can reduce stress levels, improve mental health, and promote a healthier work-life balance. This benefits employees and supports organizational success by lowering turnover, improving morale, and increasing productivity.

Enhanced Customer Satisfaction

When employees are engaged, motivated, and feel valued, they are more likely to provide high-quality customer service and work towards meeting customer needs. This can increase customer satisfaction, loyalty, and advocacy, essential for long-term success.

Improved Financial Performance

Companies with strong employee engagement and positive workplace cultures have better financial performance. Engaged employees are more productive, take fewer sick days, and are less likely to leave the organization, which can result in lower turnover costs and reduced recruitment and training expenses.

Increased Innovation and Creativity

A supportive and collaborative work environment can foster innovation and creativity by encouraging employees to think outside the box and share new ideas. This can lead to the development of new products, services, and processes, helping organizations stay ahead of the competition.

Better Risk Management

When employees feel supported and valued, they are more likely to speak up and share concerns, leading to better risk management and reduced workplace accidents and incidents.

Stronger Reputation

Companies with positive workplace cultures and high employee engagement tend to have a better reputation, making attracting new customers and employees easier.

A positive and supportive workplace culture is essential for organizational growth and success. Organizations can improve employee satisfaction, reduce turnover, and enhance performance by fostering employee engagement, promoting professional development and growth, and encouraging collaboration and teamwork. This, in turn, can lead to increased productivity, improved problem-solving and decision-making capabilities, and a healthier work-life balance, ultimately contributing to the organization's overall success.

Illustrating through practical examples

This Automobile giant has implemented several best practices to create a supportive and engaging work environment for its employees. The company understands the importance of investing in employee well-being and engagement and impacting the organization's success and growth.

It's positive workplace culture has helped to attract and retain top talent. In addition, the company values its employees and provides them with professional development and growth opportunities. This has made It an attractive place to work and has contributed to the company's success.

One of it's core values is employee engagement. The company encourages employees to be involved and take pride in their contributions. This has resulted in higher levels of job satisfaction, which has, in turn, improved employee productivity and performance. In addition, the company's positive workplace culture has fostered collaboration and teamwork, leading to more effective problem-solving and decision-making capabilities.

The company places a strong emphasis on employee well-being and health. It provides a supportive work environment that reduces stress, improves mental health, and promotes a healthier work-life balance. This has benefited employees and supported organizational success by lowering turnover, improving morale, and increasing productivity.

It's commitment to employee engagement and well-being has enhanced customer satisfaction. As a result, the company's employees provide high-quality customer service and work towards meeting customer needs, leading to increased customer satisfaction, loyalty, and advocacy.

The company's focus on employee engagement and well-being has also improved financial performance. Engaged employees are more productive, take fewer sick days, and are less likely to leave the organization, reducing turnover costs and recruitment and training expenses.

It's supportive and collaborative work environment has also encouraged innovation and creativity. Employees are encouraged to think outside the box and share new ideas, leading to the development of new products and processes. This has helped the company stay ahead of the competition.

Regarding risk management, it's employees feel supported and valued and are likelier to speak up and share concerns. This has led to better risk management and reduced workplace accidents and incidents.

The company's positive workplace culture and high employee engagement have resulted in a more substantial reputation. It is now known as an organization that values its employees, making attracting new customers and employees easier.

It's investment in employee well-being and engagement has resulted in a positive and supportive work environment that has improved employee satisfaction, reduced turnover, and enhanced performance. This, in turn, has contributed to the organization's overall success. As a result, the company serves as a real-life example of the benefits of creating a positive workplace culture and its impact on organizational success.

Take your time and try to answer these questions.

1) How does their focus on employee well-being and engagement contribute to its success?

2) Can you describe the impact of their positive workplace culture on employee satisfaction and motivation?

3) How has it's emphasis on collaboration and teamwork affected productivity and problem-solving capabilities within the company?

4) How has it's commitment to employee health and well-being improved morale and reduced turnover?

5) Can you discuss the role of employee engagement and customer satisfaction in it's financial performance?

6) How has it's supportive work environment fostered innovation and creativity within the company?

7) How has it's open communication and transparency culture improved risk management and prevented workplace accidents and incidents?

8) How has it's positive workplace culture and high employee engagement affected its reputation and ability to attract new customers and employees?

9) Can you provide examples of specific initiatives or programs that it has implemented to promote employee well-being and engagement?

10) How has it's focus on employee engagement and well-being affected its overall success and contributed to its long-term growth?

How can it work for you?

It highlights the importance of investing in employee well-being and engagement for organizational success. The leadership team of any organization can interpret this as a model for creating a supportive and positive work environment that benefits both employees and the organization as a whole.

To begin, the leadership team can analyze the impact of a positive workplace culture on employee satisfaction, motivation, and performance. By fostering a culture that values and respects employees, the organization can attract and retain top talent, improve job satisfaction, and increase engagement and productivity.

The leadership team can explore the benefits of encouraging collaboration and teamwork within the organization. As a result, the organization can improve problem-solving and decision-making capabilities and increase overall productivity by creating an environment that supports and encourages employees to work together.

Furthermore, the leadership team can assess the impact of prioritizing employee health and well-being on morale and turnover. By reducing stress levels and promoting a healthier work-life balance, the organization can improve employee satisfaction and reduce turnover, ultimately contributing to the organization's success.

The leadership team can evaluate the role of employee engagement and customer satisfaction in financial performance. By providing high-quality customer service and meeting customer needs, engaged employees can increase customer satisfaction and loyalty, leading to better financial performance for the organization.

It's case study highlights the importance of creating a positive workplace culture that values collaboration, employee well-being, and customer satisfaction. By adopting a similar approach, organizations can foster a productive and engaged workforce that is committed to achieving organizational goals. By investing in employee development, promoting work-life balance, and recognizing employee contributions, organizations can build a culture that attracts and retains top talent. By prioritizing employee and customer satisfaction, organizations can establish a competitive edge in the market and achieve long-term success.

The Growth Matrix

By considering these key takeaways from the case study of It, the leadership team can evaluate the opportunities for creating a positive workplace culture within their organization and implement specific initiatives and programs to promote employee well-being and engagement. Ultimately, this will contribute to the success and growth of the organization in the long term.

Areas of Assessment	Strengths	Weakness	Opportunities for improvement	Measurable Outcome	Action
Workplace Culture					
Employee Development					
Employee Well-being					
Employee Engagement					
Teamwork and Collaboration					

Organizations can use the below table to assess their current status in each area and identify improvement opportunities. The measurable outcomes and actionable steps can then be used to create a comprehensive improvement plan to enhance employee well-being and engagement. In addition, by regularly assessing and improving in these areas, organizations can create a collaborative and supportive work environment that drives success and growth.

Following these steps, you can create a positive and productive workplace culture that drives organizational success and enhances employee well-being. So why wait? Start making positive changes to your workplace culture today!

Innovation for Growth

> *"Embracing innovation starts with creating a supportive environment for new ideas, investing in research and development, and continuously improving products, services, and processes with the help of new technologies."*

Picture this: you're strolling through a beautiful farm in Carpendale, Queensland, Australia, surrounded by rows of luscious fruits and vegetables. As you chat with the friendly farmers about their brand and marketing strategy, you can't help but wonder how they manage to grow such amazing produce. The answer lies in their innovative approach to farming.

Firstly, they empower employees to take ownership of their work and encourage them to explore new ideas. This has led to implementing agile methodologies, such as lean and design thinking, which help farmers quickly identify and implement new ideas for their farms.

Do farmers have agile methodologies?

Yes, it is great to see farmers embracing agile methodologies in their work. Agile methodologies are typically associated with software development, but they can be applied to many different types of work, including farming.

Farmers can adopt agile practices using "agile farming." Agile farming involves breaking down tasks into smaller, more manageable pieces and working on them in short iterations. This approach allows farmers to be more flexible and adaptable, which can be particularly useful when dealing with unpredictable weather or other factors impacting crop yields.

For example, farmers using agile farming might break their planting and harvesting activities into smaller cycles, such as weekly or bi-weekly, instead of planning out an entire season's worth of crops in advance. This allows them to respond more quickly to weather patterns or other factors impacting crop growth.

Farmers using agile farming may also use data analysis to track their progress and identify areas for improvement. For example, they might use sensors to monitor soil moisture levels or track the growth rates of their crops. By collecting and analyzing this data, farmers can make more informed decisions about when to plant, harvest, or irrigate their crops, ultimately leading to higher yields and more efficient use of resources.

Their open communication and collaboration across teams and departments have fostered a culture of innovation where everyone is encouraged to share ideas and feedback. By incorporating customer feedback into their innovation process, they can create products and services that meet the needs of their customers.

The farmers also invest in research and development to continuously improve their farming processes, which has led to adopting new technologies that streamline their operations and increase efficiency. This has freed up resources that can be invested in expanding into new markets or developing new products.

But the most refreshing aspect of their innovative approach is their embrace of failure. They understand that not all ideas will be successful, but by learning from their failures, they can continuously improve and drive growth.

This organic farming team in Carpendale, Queensland, Australia, has embraced innovation by empowering their employees, promoting open communication, investing in research and development, adopting new technologies, and embracing failure. By doing so, they have set themselves apart from the competition, increased efficiency, and driven growth while growing some of the best fruits and vegetables you've ever tasted!

Organizations are always looking for ways to improve and grow; many crucial strategies can help them achieve this. Innovation is one of the strategies that help organizational growth.

Innovation plays a crucial role in the growth and success of businesses and organizations. It involves encouraging a culture that values new ideas, investing in research and development, and continuously improving products, services, and processes. By embracing innovation, organizations can set themselves apart, increase efficiency, and drive growth.

A culture of innovation starts with leadership. Organizations that prioritize innovation have leaders who actively encourage and support new ideas. This can involve creating opportunities for employees to share ideas, such as suggestion boxes or regular brainstorming sessions. Leaders can also create an environment that rewards risk-taking and experimentation, recognizing that not all pictures will succeed.

Investing in research and development is another critical aspect of fostering innovation. This can involve setting aside a budget for new product development or exploring new technologies to improve existing products or processes. Companies can also collaborate with universities, research institutes, and other organizations to access cutting-edge technology and research.

Innovation can also involve improving existing products, services, and processes. This can include conducting regular assessments to identify areas for improvement and implementing changes to increase efficiency. For example, a company might use data analysis to identify bottlenecks in its supply chain and make changes to reduce lead times.

Innovation can also help organizations differentiate themselves from the competition. The company should invest in developing new products or technologies that can offer unique solutions that competitors cannot match. This can help organizations build a loyal customer base and increase market share.

Innovation can also drive growth by increasing efficiency. For example, a company that invests in new technologies to streamline processes can reduce costs and increase productivity. This can free up resources that can be invested in other business areas, such as expanding into new markets or developing new products.

Employee Empowerment

Encouraging employees to take ownership of their work and giving them the tools and resources they need to innovate can help organizations drive growth. Organizations should provide training opportunities and allow employees to explore new ideas and approaches.

Open Communication

Encouraging open communication and collaboration across teams and departments can foster a culture of innovation. This can involve creating opportunities for employees to share ideas and feedback and promoting a culture of transparency and honesty.

Agile Methodologies

Adopting agile methodologies, such as lean or design thinking, can help organizations quickly identify and implement new ideas. These methodologies emphasize rapid iteration and continuous improvement and can help organizations respond rapidly to changes in the market.

Customer Feedback

Incorporating customer feedback into the innovation process can help organizations create products and services that meet the needs of their customers. This can involve regularly conducting customer surveys and focus groups and using the information gathered to inform product development and process improvement efforts.

Embracing Failure

Fostering a culture that embraces failure as an opportunity to learn and grow is essential for innovation.

Organizations can encourage employees to take risks and experiment, knowing that not all ideas will be successful. By learning from failures, organizations can continuously improve and drive growth.

Technology Adoption

Embracing new technologies can help organizations improve processes, increase efficiency, and drive growth. Organizations should adopt automation technologies to streamline processes or cloud-based solutions to increase collaboration and flexibility.

Market Monitoring

Monitoring market trends and competitor activity is essential for staying ahead in the innovation game. Organizations can use this information to identify new opportunities and stay ahead of the competition by continuously improving products, services, and processes.

Innovation is a crucial component of an organization's growth and success. By encouraging a culture of innovation, investing in research and development, and continuously improving products, services, and processes, organizations can set themselves apart from the competition, increase efficiency, and drive growth. Additionally, organizations can foster a culture of innovation that drives success by empowering employees, promoting open communication, embracing new technologies, and monitoring market trends.

Illustrating through practical examples

Innovation is crucial for growth and success in any industry, including hospitality. One company that has successfully embraced innovation and achieved significant growth is this American chain of hotels & resorts, a leading player in the hospitality industry that has a rich history of continuously improving its products and services. By doing so, they have been able to stay ahead of the competition and establish themselves as one of the largest hotel chains in the world.

This American chain of hotels & resorts strongly focuses on innovation, with a culture that values new ideas and encourages employees to share their thoughts and suggestions. This culture starts with leadership, with senior executives actively seeking and encouraging new ideas from employees. It has also invested heavily in research and development, regularly setting aside a budget for new product development and exploring new technologies to improve existing products or processes.

One key area where it has embraced innovation is in their customer experience. They regularly conduct customer surveys and focus groups to gather feedback and insights, which they then use to inform product development and process improvement efforts. This has led to several innovations in the hospitality industry, such as the introduction of their mobile check-in and check-out service, which allows guests to skip the front desk and go straight to their rooms. This service has been a massive hit with guests, with data showing that more than 60% of It's guests now use the mobile check-in and check-out service.

It has also embraced technology in a big way, adopting automation technologies to streamline processes and cloud-based solutions to increase collaboration and flexibility. For example, they were one of the first hotel chains to introduce voice-activated room controls, allowing guests to control the room's temperature, lighting, and TV with voice commands. Guests have received this innovation well, with data showing that more than 75% of It guests now use voice-activated room controls.

It is also an agile organization, using lean and design thinking methodologies to quickly identify and implement new ideas. This has allowed them to respond rapidly to changes in the market and stay ahead of the competition. For example, they promptly responded to the rise of home-sharing platforms by introducing their home-sharing platform. This platform allows guests to book unique and luxurious vacation homes and villas and has been a massive hit with guests, with data showing that bookings on the forum have increased by more than 50% in the past year.

In conclusion, This American chain of hotels & resorts is an excellent example of how embracing innovation can drive growth and success in the hospitality industry. By fostering a culture of innovation, investing in research and development, and continuously improving products, services, and processes, it has set itself apart from the competition, increased efficiency, and driven growth. Additionally, by empowering employees, promoting open communication, embracing new technologies, and monitoring market trends, it has created a culture of innovation that drives success.

Innovation for Growth

Take your time and try to answer these questions.

1) Describe the measures this American chain of hotels & resorts took to establish an innovative culture within the organization.

2) How did it's leaders encourage and support new ideas from employees?

3) Explain it's research and development investments and their impact on the company's growth.

4) Discuss how it integrated customer feedback into their innovation process.

5) Elaborate on it's approach to viewing failure as a learning opportunity.

6) How has it's adoption of new technologies impacted its processes and efficiency?

7) Can you discuss it's approach to monitoring market trends and staying ahead of the competition?

8) Discuss how it's focus on innovation has helped them stand out from competitors and drive growth.

9) Explain the significance of employee empowerment in It's innovative culture.

10) Describe it's approach to fostering open communication and collaboration across departments.

How can it work for you?

The case study of this American chain of hotels & resorts highlights several key strategies that organizations can adopt to foster a culture of innovation and drive growth. The leadership team can consider the following steps to interpret and apply this information to their organization.

Establishing a supportive environment for innovation is critical for organizations to foster a culture of innovation. Encouraging and rewarding employees for new ideas can motivate them to develop more innovative ideas. Organizations can create opportunities for collaboration and brainstorming sessions where employees can share their thoughts and develop new and innovative ideas. Additionally, providing training and resources to support innovation can equip employees with the necessary skills and knowledge to drive innovation.

Investing in research and development can be a crucial strategy for organizations to drive growth. Setting aside a budget for new product development and exploring new technologies to improve existing products or processes is vital. Collaborating with other organizations to access cutting-edge technology and research can also bring fresh perspectives and help organizations stay ahead of the competition.

Continuous improvement is a must for organizations that want to drive growth. Conducting regular assessments to identify areas for improvement and implementing changes to increase efficiency is essential. Additionally, investing in developing new products or technologies can help organizations stay ahead of the competition and drive growth.

Embracing failure as a learning opportunity is another strategy that organizations can adopt. Fostering a culture that views failure as an opportunity to learn and grow can encourage employees to take risks and experiment. By embracing failure, organizations can learn from their mistakes and improve their processes and products.

Integrating customer feedback can help organizations stay in touch with their customers and understand their needs and preferences. In addition, regularly gathering customer feedback and using it to inform product development and process improvement efforts can help organizations stay ahead of the competition and improve customer satisfaction.

Embracing new technologies is another critical strategy for organizations to drive growth. Adopting new technologies to streamline processes, increase efficiency, and drive change is crucial for organizations to stay ahead of the competition.

Monitoring market trends is essential for organizations that want to stay ahead of the competition. Staying informed about market trends and competitor activity can help organizations improve their products, services, and processes and stay ahead of the competition.

Empowering employees is crucial for organizations that want to foster innovation. Encouraging employees to take ownership of their work and providing them with the tools and resources they need to innovate can help organizations drive innovation and growth.

Promoting open communication and collaboration is another critical strategy for organizations to drive growth. Creating opportunities for employees to share ideas and feedback and promoting a culture of transparency and honesty can help organizations improve processes and products and drive growth.

Adopting agile methodologies, such as lean or design thinking, is another strategy organizations can adopt. Emphasizing rapid iteration and continuous improvement can help organizations stay ahead of the competition and drive growth. Organizations can continuously improve processes and products by adopting agile methodologies and driving innovation and growth.

Areas of Assessment	Evaluation	Strengths	Weakness	Measurable Outcome	Action
Environment of Innovation					
Research and Development					
Failure as a learning opportunity					
Customer Feedback					
Adoption of New Technologies					
Market Trends					
Employee Empowerment					
Communication and Collaboration					

Organizations can use this table to fill in the Evaluation and Strength/Weakness columns based on their current state. Then, they can develop a Measurable & Actionable Approach for each category to address their weaknesses and build upon their strengths. Finally, this information can be compiled into a report summarizing the organization's current state and providing a roadmap for improvement.

If you're looking to drive growth and foster a culture of innovation in your organization, consider taking inspiration from the success of this American chain of hotels & resorts. By following key strategies such as establishing a supportive environment for innovation, investing in R&D, embracing failure as a learning opportunity, and monitoring market trends, you can drive growth and promote a culture of innovation. We encourage you to look at these strategies and consider how to apply them in your organization. With a measured and actionable approach, you can drive positive change and achieve success, and open to helping and supporting you in your efforts to drive innovation and growth in your organization.

The Growth Matrix

Diversification for Growth

"Diversification is the key to unlocking organizational growth and mitigating risk by expanding product and service offerings into new markets and industries."

Sweet Delights, an Anglo-Indian family-owned bakery, had built a reputation for its delectable cakes and pastries over 20 years in my native town. The owners, Britto and Annie, were my friends then and rarely talked as I moved away for the past 10 years. However, in recent years, the business has been experiencing a decline in sales due to changing market trends and increased competition. Sensing the need for adaptation, the owners, Britto and Annie, approached me for help to ensure their business's long-term success.

After conducting thorough market research and analysis, we identified the potential for growth through diversification. Expanding their product offerings could reduce their reliance on cakes and pastries and increase their revenue streams. We explored the catering industry and identified a growing demand for catered events in their local area, such as weddings and corporate functions.

Using my network, I connected Britto and Annie to a local event planner, Edward, who had extensive experience in the catering industry. They collaborated to develop a menu that would be a perfect fit for events of all sizes and budgets. Edward requested that Sweet Delights provide a high-quality product with a competitive price on time, and both parties agreed.

Sweet Delights began offering catering services, starting with birthday parties and family gatherings and gradually expanding to more significant events like weddings and corporate functions. With Edward's help, Sweet Delights quickly became known for its delicious and high-quality food offerings.

We integrated diversification into Sweet Delights' strategic plan, allocating resources effectively and continuously monitoring and evaluating their performance to identify areas of improvement and make necessary adjustments. Within a year, the catering business had grown so much that a separate division, Sweet Delights Catering, was required to manage the demand. Britto focused on the bakery, while Annie looked after the catering business, maintaining a healthy balance.

Sweet Delights' story demonstrates the effectiveness of diversification as a growth strategy for businesses seeking to adapt to changing market trends and reduce dependence on a single product or market. By collaborating with local experts, conducting thorough market research, and taking a strategic approach, Britto and Annie were able to expand their business and achieve long-term success.

Recently, Annie informed me they are now taking tenders to supply cakes and bread to government hospitals. Britto has expanded to supply catering services to major IT companies in and around their area. I am working with them to expand their network with a franchisee model, and it is evident that growth is inevitable for Sweet Delights.

Diversification - The business world constantly evolves, and organizations must adapt to these changes to ensure long-term success. Diversification is a strategic approach that enables organizations to expand their product or service offerings into new markets and industries, reducing dependence on a single product or market and increasing revenue. As a result, organizations can mitigate risk, improve competitiveness, and drive maximum growth by diversifying their operations.

Diversification is an organization's strategic approach to drive growth and mitigate risk by expanding its product or service offerings into new markets, industries, and business opportunities. This approach helps organizations reduce dependence on a single product or market, increase revenue, and improve competitiveness. In the context of organizational growth, diversification is crucial for maximizing growth and ensuring the long-term stability and success of the business.

One of the critical benefits of diversification is the reduction of dependence on a single product or market. This means that if one product or market experiences a downturn, the organization is less likely to be severely impacted, as they have other products or needs to rely on. This helps to reduce the overall risk of the business and provides a more stable source of revenue. Moreover, diversifying into new markets and industries can also provide growth opportunities, as organizations can tap into new customer segments and access new resources and expertise. This can lead to increased revenue and a more robust overall business model.

Another important aspect of diversification is increased competitiveness. Organizations can gain a competitive advantage by entering new markets and industries by accessing new customers, resources, and expertise. Additionally, diversification can lead to developing new products and services, giving organizations a unique selling proposition and differentiating them from their competitors. This can help organizations to achieve a competitive edge in the market and increase their overall market share.

Moreover, diversification can also help organizations better manage and respond to market changes. For example, if a particular market experiences a downturn, organizations that have diversified into other markets are more likely to be able to weather the storm and continue to grow. This is because they have a more diverse and resilient business model better equipped to respond to market changes. Additionally, by diversifying their operations, organizations can better manage risk and minimize the impact of market changes on their overall business.

Another significant benefit of diversification is increased revenue. Organizations can access new customers and revenue streams by entering new markets and industries. This can increase overall revenue and improve the business's financial stability. Furthermore, by diversifying their operations, organizations can leverage economies of scale and realize cost savings. This can also contribute to increased revenue and profitability.

Diversification is essential for organizations seeking to drive growth and mitigate risk. By expanding their product or service offerings into new markets and industries, organizations can reduce dependence on a single product or market, increase revenue, and improve their overall competitiveness. Additionally, diversification can help organizations manage market changes better, minimize risk, and achieve maximum growth. Therefore, organizations should consider diversification a key component of their growth strategy.

Market research and analysis: Before diversifying into new markets, organizations must conduct thorough market research and analysis to understand the potential opportunities and challenges in the target market. This will help organizations to make informed decisions and avoid costly mistakes.

Collaboration and partnerships: Diversifying into new markets often requires teamwork and partnerships with local organizations and experts. This can help organizations leverage local partners' knowledge and resources, increase their success chances, and overcome cultural or language barriers.

Strategic planning: Diversification should be integrated into the organization's overall strategic plan and align with its mission, vision, and values. A well-defined strategy can help organizations to focus their efforts, allocate resources effectively, and achieve their desired outcomes.

Gradual and controlled growth: Diversification should be approached gradually and with control to minimize risk and ensure the sustainability of the business. Organizations should start with a small and manageable investment, test the waters, and expand gradually as they gain experience and confidence in the new market.

Continuous monitoring and evaluation: Diversification is not a one-time effort but a continuous monitoring and evaluation process. Organizations should regularly assess the performance of their diversified operations, identify areas of improvement, and make necessary adjustments to ensure maximum growth and profitability.

These are some additional key elements and strategies that organizations can consider as they embark on the diversification journey. By taking a strategic and well-planned approach to diversification, organizations can increase their chances of success and achieve long-term growth and stability.

Illustrating through practical examples

Diversification is an organization's strategic approach to drive growth and mitigate risk by expanding its product or service offerings into new markets, industries, and business opportunities. The system helps organizations reduce dependence on a single product or market, increase revenue, and improve competitiveness. This article will explore the importance of diversification in organizational growth through a real-life case study of a multinational organization.

The company in question is a leading multinational conglomerate that operates in several industries, including technology, retail, and finance. The company has a long history of success, but over the years, it has become heavily dependent on its technology division, which accounts for a significant portion of its revenue. The company's management realized that relying too heavily on a single product or market could be risky and decided to diversify its operations to mitigate that risk and drive growth.

The first step in the diversification process was market research and analysis. The company thoroughly studied potential new markets and industries and identified several expansion opportunities. The company then focused on one of the most promising opportunities: the retail industry. The company's management realized that the retail sector was a growing market with high growth potential, and there was a market gap for a technology-driven retail solution.

The next step was collaborating and forming partnerships with local organizations and experts. For example, the company partnered with a leading retail company in the target market and leveraged its expertise and resources to gain a competitive advantage. The partnership also allowed the company to overcome cultural or language barriers and better understand the local market.

The company then developed a strategic plan to diversify into the retail industry. The project included a gradual and controlled approach to growth, focusing on testing the waters and gradually expanding as the company gained experience and confidence in the new market. The company also allocated sufficient resources for the new venture, including personnel, technology, and marketing efforts.

The company's diversification into the retail industry was a success. The company leveraged its technical expertise to create a unique and innovative retail solution that differentiated it from its competitors. The company's technology-driven approach to retail attracted a new customer base and helped it to increase its market share in the retail industry. The company's retail division quickly became a significant contributor to its overall revenue and helped to reduce its dependence on its technology division.

The company continued to monitor and evaluate its diversified operations and made necessary adjustments to ensure maximum growth and profitability. The company also continued diversifying into other markets and industries, leveraging its experience and expertise to succeed in these new ventures. Today, the company is a well-diversified multinational conglomerate with a strong presence in several sectors and a more robust and resilient business model.

The case of the multinational conglomerate demonstrates the importance of diversification in organizational growth. The company's diversification into the retail industry reduced its dependence on a single product or market, increased revenue, and improved its competitiveness. By taking a strategic and well-planned approach to diversification, the company achieved maximum growth and ensured long-term stability and success. Organizations looking to drive growth and mitigate risk should consider diversification a key component of their overall growth strategy.

Take your time and try to answer these questions.

1) Can you explain the concept of diversification and its benefits for organizational growth?

2) How did the multinational company in the case study apply the diversification strategy to expand its business and drive growth?

3) How did the company's diversification efforts contribute to reducing its dependence on a single product or market?

4) Can you provide examples of how the company's diversification led to increased competitiveness and a more resilient business model?

5) How did the company manage and respond to market changes due to its diversification strategy?

6) Discuss the impact of diversification on the company's revenue and profitability.

7) How did the company leverage economies of scale and realize cost savings through diversification?

8) Identify the key factors that contributed to the success of the company's diversification strategy.

9) What lessons can be learned from this case study, and how can they be applied to your organization?

10) How can your organization implement a diversification strategy to drive growth and mitigate risk?

How can it work for you?

Interpreting the case study in their organization can provide valuable insights and lessons for the leadership team. For example, they can use the case study to understand how diversification drives growth and mitigates risk. The following steps can help them to interpret the case study and apply its lessons to their organization.

Analyzing the business model is an essential first step in an organization's diversification process. The leadership team should assess their current business model and identify areas where diversification can bring benefits, such as reducing dependence on a single product or market and improving competitiveness. This step is crucial in determining where the organization can improve and grow through diversification.

Assessing market opportunities is the next step in the process. The team should thoroughly evaluate the market opportunities available to their organization, including new industries and customer segments. This will help them identify potential areas for diversification and determine the best course of action. By understanding the market opportunities, the organization can make informed decisions about which areas to pursue and how to maximize the benefits of diversification.

Once the market opportunities have been assessed, developing a diversification strategy is next. The leadership team should develop a diversification strategy aligning with their business goals and objectives. This strategy should outline the organization's steps to diversify its operations and the resources required. By having a clear and well-defined process in place, the organization can ensure that they are taking the proper steps to achieve its goals and maximize the benefits of diversification.

Implementing the diversification strategy is the next step in the process. The leadership team should take the necessary steps to expand their product or service offerings into new markets, such as acquiring new businesses or entering into strategic partnerships. This step is crucial in ensuring the organization can achieve the desired results from diversification and implement the strategy effectively. The team should ensure that the implementation of the system is well-planned and that the necessary resources are in place to support it.

Monitoring and adjusting the diversification strategy is essential to ensure it delivers the desired results and aligns with changing market conditions. Therefore, the team should regularly assess the strategy's progress and make necessary adjustments to ensure it meets its goals and delivers the desired results. By continuously monitoring and adjusting the process, the organization can ensure that they are taking the proper steps to achieve its goals and maximize the benefits of diversification.

Evaluating the results of the diversification strategy is essential to ensure that it delivers the desired results and identifies improvement areas. The leadership team should assess the impact of the diversification strategy on revenue and profitability and identify areas where they can make improvements. By evaluating the results, the organization can determine the effectiveness of its design and make any necessary adjustments to ensure that they maximize the benefits of diversification

Organizational Diversification Assessment Table

Strengths:
- *Current Business Model:*
- *Areas of strength*
- *Unique selling proposition*
- *Competitive edge*

Weaknesses:

- *Dependence on a single product or market*
- *Limited revenue streams*
- *Lack of market diversification*

Opportunities:

- *New markets and industries*
- *Customer segments*
- *Access to new resources and expertise*

Threats:

- *Market changes*
- *Competition*
- *Economic conditions*

Actionable Approach:

- *Analyze the current business model*
- *Assess market opportunities*
- *Develop a diversification strategy*
- *Implement the strategy*
- *Monitor and adjust the strategy*
- *Evaluate the results*

Measurement:

- *Reduction in dependence on a single product or market*
- *Increased revenue and profitability*
- *Improved competitiveness*
- *Diverse and resilient business model*

Based on the assessment, organizations can identify their strengths and weaknesses in diversification and develop a strategy that leverages and addresses their shortcomings. The actionable approach provides a roadmap for implementing the plan and continuously monitoring and adjusting it to ensure its success. The measurement offers a way to track progress and evaluate the results, allowing organizations to make data-driven decisions and maximize the benefits of diversification.

Criteria	Evaluation	Strengths	Weakness	Actionable Steps
Business Model				
Market Opportunities				
Diversification Strategy				
Implementation				
Monitoring				
Evaluation				
Employee Empowerment				
Communication and Collaboration				

The above table provides a clear and actionable approach for organizations to assess and implement their diversification strategy. By evaluating their business model, market opportunities, and diversification strategy, organizations can ensure they are on the right track to maximize growth and mitigate risk. In addition, regular monitoring and evaluation of the results will help organizations continuously improve their diversification strategy and business growth.

We want to encourage organizations to take advantage of the benefits of diversification, and by doing so, organizations can ensure their long-term success and drive maximum growth.

Digital Transformation for Growth

"Don't be a sourpuss in a sweet world of technology — embrace digital transformation, or risk getting stuck in the past while everyone else sips on the tasty, sweetened business coffee of success."

In early 2021, I was approached by a pharmaceutical marketing company that specializes in gastroenterology, gynecology, diabetic, and orthopedic industries. The company's management had recognized the need to transform their business to remain competitive in the rapidly changing digital landscape. They asked me to help them implement a digital transformation strategy that would help them streamline their operations, increase efficiency, and enhance customer experience. They understood that technology could drive change and create new opportunities, so we set out to integrate digital solutions into all business areas.

By automating manual processes and streamlining workflows, we reduced the time and resources required to complete tasks. This improved productivity and reduced costs, which we reinvested into other areas of their business. As a result, their sales representatives could focus on building relationships with healthcare providers. In contrast, their operations team had more time to develop new products and improve existing ones.

Digital solutions also helped them use data and analytics better, improving our decision-making and providing a better understanding of customer needs and preferences. This was especially important for their sales representatives, who could tailor their presentations to individual healthcare providers based on their prescribing history and patient demographics.

We also focused on enhancing the customer experience by offering a more personalized and convenient experience through digital solutions. For example, healthcare providers could access product information and educational resources through the company website. In addition, we developed a mobile application that allowed them to place orders and track their deliveries easily.

We must upskill and reskill our employees to successfully implement a digital transformation. We recommended that the company invest in training and development programs to ensure employees have the skills and knowledge to use new technologies effectively. The sales representatives were trained to place orders and track deliveries using our mobile application. We trained their operations team to use new data analytics tools to improve product development.

Of course, we also faced challenges along the way. One of the biggest challenges was ensuring that digital solutions were integrated effectively across our organization. We had to work closely with different departments and teams to ensure everyone was on board and the technology was being used effectively.

But despite the challenges, the benefits of digital transformation were clear. By embracing technology and upskilling the employees, we improved operations, increased efficiency, and enhanced the customer experience. The sales representatives and consulting doctors were able to experience a seamless digital experience, which made their jobs easier and provided them with the tools and resources they needed to provide better care to their patients.

I firmly believe in technology's power to drive change and create opportunities. And in today's fast-paced and ever-changing business environment, digital transformation is more important than ever.

Digital transformation refers to using technology to fundamentally change how organizations operate and deliver value to customers. It involves integrating digital technology into all business areas, fundamentally changing business operations, and delivering value to customers.

In an ever-changing business environment, organizations must be agile, flexible, and able to respond quickly to market demands. As a result, organizations can improve processes, increase productivity, and enhance the customer experience by adopting digital solutions. This leads to significant growth opportunities and a competitive advantage in the market.

One of the key benefits of digital transformation is increased efficiency. Organizations can reduce the time and resources required to complete tasks by automating manual processes and streamlining workflows. This results in improved productivity and reduced costs, which can be reinvested into other business areas. Additionally, digital solutions can help organizations to make better use of data and analytics, leading to improved decision-making and a better understanding of customer needs and preferences.

Another key benefit of digital transformation is enhanced customer experience. Organizations can offer customers a more personalized and convenient experience by adopting digital solutions, regardless of location. This can help to build stronger customer relationships and increase customer loyalty, leading to long-term growth and success.

Organizations must have a clear and well-defined strategy to implement a digital transformation successfully. This includes identifying the areas of the business that need improvement and the specific technologies that will help to achieve this. It also involves engaging with employees, partners, and customers to ensure that everyone understands the benefits of digital transformation and is on board with the change.

One of the biggest challenges facing organizations as they embark on digital transformation is the need to upskill and reskill employees. As new technologies are introduced, employees must be trained to use them effectively. This requires a significant investment in training and development, but it is essential if organizations are to achieve their digital transformation goals.

Another challenge is ensuring that digital solutions are integrated effectively across the organization. This requires a deep understanding of the organization's processes and systems and close collaboration between departments and teams. Organizations need to be able to work together seamlessly to achieve their digital transformation goals.

Despite the challenges, the benefits of digital transformation are clear. Organizations can grow much bigger and better by leveraging technology to improve operations, increase efficiency, and enhance customer experiences. As a result, a digital transformation is no longer an option but a necessity for organizations that want to remain competitive and succeed in the long term.

Cybersecurity: As organizations become more digitally connected, they are more vulnerable to cyber-attacks. Therefore, it is crucial to have strong cybersecurity measures in place to protect sensitive data and prevent breaches.

Cloud Computing: Cloud-based solutions are becoming increasingly popular as they offer scalability, flexibility, and cost savings. Organizations should consider leveraging cloud computing to streamline their operations and improve efficiency.

Agility: Digital transformation is not a one-time project but an ongoing journey. Therefore, organizations must adopt an agile mindset to respond quickly to changing business needs and technological advancements.

Change Management: Digital transformation involves significant changes to how organizations operate, which can be challenging for employees. Therefore, it is essential to have a change management plan in place to communicate the changes effectively and ensure buy-in from all stakeholders.

Digital transformation is a complex and challenging process, but it is essential for organizations that want to remain competitive and grow. The key to success is having a clear and well-defined strategy and ensuring that digital solutions are integrated effectively across the organization.

Remember, digital transformation is not just a buzzword but a critical aspect of modern business. By embracing technology and upskilling employees, organizations can improve processes, increase efficiency, and enhance the customer experience, leading to significant growth opportunities and a competitive advantage in the market.

Illustrating through practical examples

In recent years, the Logistics and Supply Chain industry has undergone a significant transformation with the advent of new technologies. The rise of digital transformation has enabled organizations in this industry to optimize their operations and enhance the customer experience, leading to improved growth and success. One such organization that has successfully implemented a digital transformation is The German Logistic Company.

This German Logistic Company is a global logistics company that provides transportation, warehousing, and supply chain management services to clients across various industries. It recognized the need to adopt digital solutions to improve its operations and deliver a better customer experience to remain competitive in a rapidly changing business environment.

To achieve this, it embarked on a digital transformation journey that involved integrating digital technology into all areas of its business. This included implementing a centralized information management system that allowed for real-time tracking and monitoring of shipments and advanced analytics to optimize supply chain processes.

Additionally, it invested in new technologies such as robotics and automation, which enabled the company to reduce manual labor and increase efficiency. For example, it implemented a robotics system that automated the sorting and distribution of packages in its warehouses, significantly increasing productivity and reducing errors.

To ensure that employees were equipped with the skills and knowledge needed to use these new technologies effectively, it invested heavily in training and development programs. This included providing employees access to online training resources and offering in-person training sessions focused on using new technologies and data analysis.

Implementing these digital solutions significantly improved It's operations and customer experience. By using advanced analytics, it was able to identify areas of its supply chain that needed improvement and take corrective action, resulting in reduced delivery times and increased customer satisfaction. Additionally, using robotics and automation led to a significant increase in productivity and reduced costs.

Robotics and Automation: It has implemented robotics and automation to streamline its supply chain operations, reduce errors, and increase efficiency. For instance, they have deployed autonomous mobile robots to transport packages in their warehouses, reducing the time required to move goods and improving safety.

Internet of Things (IoT): It has implemented IoT technologies to improve supply chain visibility and real-time tracking of goods. For example, they have developed IoT sensors that provide real-time temperature monitoring for sensitive products, ensuring they are transported at the right temperature.

Digital Twin: It has created digital twins of their warehouses and other facilities to simulate and optimize their operations. This helps them identify areas for improvement and test new solutions before implementing them in real-world scenarios.

Blockchain: It uses blockchain technology to improve supply chain transparency and security. They have developed a blockchain-based platform that allows stakeholders to track and verify the origin and authenticity of goods, ensuring they are not counterfeit.

It's digital transformation initiatives focus on improving their operations, increasing efficiency, and enhancing the customer experience through technology adoption. It has been a resounding success, enabling the company to remain competitive in a rapidly changing business environment. By adopting digital solutions and upskilling employees, It was able to optimize its operations and enhance the customer experience, leading to significant growth opportunities and a competitive advantage in the market.

The Logistics and Supply Chain industry is rapidly changing, and organizations that want to remain competitive need to embrace digital transformation. By following a clear and well-defined strategy and investing in new technologies and employee upskilling, organizations can improve processes, increase efficiency, and enhance the customer experience, leading to significant growth opportunities and a competitive advantage in the market. The case of It is a testament to the power of digital transformation and the benefits it can bring to organizations across various industries.

Take your time and try to answer these questions.

1) What were the key challenges that it faced in its logistics and supply chain operations before its digital transformation?

2) How did it identify the areas of their business that needed improvement, and what technologies did they implement to address them?

3) How did it ensure that digital solutions were effectively integrated across the organization?

4) What role did upskilling and reskilling play in it's digital transformation, and how did they approach employee training and development?

5) How did it's digital transformation impact its operational efficiency, productivity, and customer experience?

6) How did it's digital transformation give them a competitive advantage in the market, and what benefits did it bring to the company in the long term?

7) What lessons can other organizations learn from it's digital transformation journey, and how can they apply them to their business?

How can it work for you?

After reviewing the it case study, an organization's leadership team can take the following steps to interpret the lessons learned and apply them to your business.

Assess current processes and systems: The organization should begin by identifying areas of their business that need improvement, such as inefficient processes, outdated technology, or poor customer experiences. This can be done through surveys, feedback from customers and employees, or data analysis.

Develop a clear digital transformation strategy: Once the areas for improvement have been identified, the organization should develop a clear digital transformation strategy that outlines the specific technologies and solutions that will be implemented to address these areas. This strategy should also include a timeline for implementation and an evaluation plan to measure the effectiveness of the digital transformation.

Communicate the benefits of digital transformation to employees and stakeholders: The leadership team needs to communicate the benefits of digital transformation to all stakeholders, including employees, partners, and customers. This helps ensure that everyone is on board with the changes and understands the value of digital transformation.

Invest in employee training and development: As new technologies are introduced, employees must be trained to use them effectively. Therefore, the organization should invest in employee training and development to ensure they have the necessary skills and knowledge to support digital transformation.

Ensure effective integration of digital solutions across the organization: The organization should work closely with all departments and teams to ensure that digital solutions are integrated effectively. This may require close collaboration and communication to ensure everyone is aligned with the digital transformation strategy.

Monitor and evaluate the effectiveness of the digital transformation: Once implemented, the organization should monitor and assess its effectiveness to ensure that it delivers the expected benefits. This can help identify areas needing further improvement or adjustment to ensure the organization achieves its goals.

Some questions organizations may want to consider on digital transformation are:

1) How can we ensure our digital transformation initiatives align with our business strategy and objectives?

2) Are there any emerging technologies we should explore to stay ahead of the competition and improve our operations?

3) How can we effectively measure the success of our digital transformation efforts?

4) What steps must we take to ensure we have the right talent and skills to drive our digital transformation initiatives forward?

5) How can we ensure our digital solutions are scalable and grow with our organization?

6) How can we effectively communicate the benefits of digital transformation to all stakeholders, including employees, customers, and partners?

7) What potential risks and challenges must we know as we embark on our digital transformation journey?

8) How can we foster a culture of innovation and agility to support our digital transformation efforts?

By following these steps, an organization can successfully implement a digital transformation leading to improved operational efficiency, productivity, and customer experiences. The It case study provides a valuable example of how digital transformation can lead to significant growth opportunities and a competitive advantage in the market.

Aspect	Evaluation	Strengths	Weakness	Actionable Steps
Technology				
Process				
Employee Skills				
Customer Service				
Financial Management				
Sales Operation				
Marketing				
Supply Chain				

It's important to note that this is just a sample table and should be customized to fit each organization's specific needs and goals. However, using a systematic and measurable approach, organizations can better identify their strengths and weaknesses and take actionable steps to improve overall performance and achieve their strategic objectives.

It has provided valuable insights and information on the benefits and challenges of adopting digital solutions.

As you consider your organization's digital transformation journey, I encourage you to assess your current strengths and weaknesses, develop a clear strategy, and engage your employees, partners, and customers. Remember that digital transformation is an ongoing process that requires a commitment to upskilling and reskilling your workforce as new technologies emerge.

Suppose you have any questions or want to discuss your organization's digital transformation journey further. In that case, I can help you navigate this complex and exciting journey, and we look forward to hearing from you.

The Growth Matrix

Financial Management for Growth

> *"Financial management is not just about balancing the books; it's about balancing the opportunities and risks that shape your organization's future."*

As a young entrepreneur, I dreamed of creating a successful education business. I invested all my savings and even took out loans to get started. I had a vision of offering quality education to students at an affordable price. However, I soon realized I needed more financial management skills to run a business successfully.

I made several mistakes early on, such as not correctly forecasting expenses and not negotiating favorable terms with suppliers. As a result, I struggled to pay bills, and debt began to pile up. I even borrowed money from my family to keep the business afloat.

Despite trying to turn things around, I eventually lost all my money and our ancestral properties. It was a tough time, and I had to start again from scratch.

But I didn't give up. I realized that I needed to learn from my mistakes and implement better financial management strategies to avoid repeating the same mistakes. I began by creating a well-designed financial management plan that helped me make informed decisions about allocating resources, prioritizing expenses, and planning for future growth.

I also started forecasting accurately, which allowed me to predict future revenue and expenses and plan accordingly. With a clear understanding of my organization's economic situation, I could make informed decisions about which projects to invest in, how much to spend, and how to balance the needs of different stakeholders.

I learned the importance of budgeting, created a plan for my business's financial resources, including revenue and expenses, and allocated them to achieve specific goals. I kept track of my financial goals and maximized my resources with a well-designed budget.

I also learned how to negotiate effectively, securing better deals with suppliers, customers, and other stakeholders. As a result, I was able to reduce costs, increase revenue, and ensure favorable terms for myself.

Another crucial aspect of financial management that I implemented was reducing expenses. I automated various business areas, such as invoicing, accounting, and payroll. This reduced the workload of employees and the risk of human error, which led to financial loss. Additionally, automation helped me save time and reduce costs by automating repetitive tasks, freeing employees to focus on more strategic tasks.

I cut down on unnecessary costs, reducing energy consumption, reviewing supplier contracts to ensure the best deal, and reducing the use of non-essential office supplies. I was mindful of how resources were used and made sure that they were being used in the most efficient way possible.

With these strategies in place, I was able to find new ways to generate revenue to maximize profits proactively. I diversified my product offerings, expanded into new markets, and found new ways to reach existing customers. Having a solid financial management plan, I identified areas where I could increase revenue and make informed decisions about allocating resources to achieve these goals.

I achieved financial stability by generating enough revenue, managing costs effectively, and having a solid financial plan. I proactively managed risk, reducing the risk of financial loss and protecting my bottom line.

It was an arduous journey, but by adopting sound financial practices, I achieved sustainable growth and reached new heights of success. By regularly reviewing financial statements and key performance indicators, I identified areas where I needed to make adjustments or improvements. This allowed me to make informed decisions about allocating resources and changing my financial plan to achieve my goals more effectively.

I learned that financial management is an ongoing process, and reviewed and adjust my financial plan to stay on track and adapt to changing circumstances. By being proactive and flexible, I can continue to achieve growth and sustainability over the long term.

Financial management is crucial to any organization as it effectively manages cash flow, reduces costs, and maximizes profits. This helps organizations to ensure financial stability and reduce the risk of financial loss. It is also essential in making decisions that impact the growth and sustainability of the organization.

A well-designed financial management plan will help an organization make informed decisions about allocating resources, prioritizing expenses, and planning for future growth. By clearly understanding the organization's economic situation, leaders can make informed decisions about which projects to invest in, how much to spend, and how to balance the needs of different stakeholders.

Forecasting is essential to financial management, allowing organizations to predict future revenue and expenses and plan accordingly. With accurate forecasts, organizations can make informed decisions about future investments and expenditures and allocate resources more effectively.

Budgeting is another crucial aspect of financial management. It involves creating a plan for the organization's financial resources, including revenue and expenses, and allocating them to achieve specific goals. Organizations can ensure they stay on track with their financial goals and maximize their resources by having a well-designed budget.

Negotiations are also necessary for financial management, allowing organizations to secure better deals with suppliers, customers, and other stakeholders. In addition, practical negotiation skills can help organizations reduce costs, increase revenue, and ensure favorable terms for themselves. As a result, organizations can achieve their financial goals more efficiently and sustainably by negotiating effectively.

One of the critical elements of effective financial management is reducing expenses. This can be achieved by implementing automation in various areas of the organization, such as invoicing, accounting, and payroll. Automation reduces the workload of employees and the risk of human error, which can lead to financial loss. Additionally, automation can help organizations save time and reduce costs by automating repetitive tasks, freeing employees to focus on more strategic tasks.

Another way to reduce expenses is by cutting down on unnecessary costs. This could include reducing energy consumption, reviewing supplier contracts to ensure the best deal, and reducing the use of non-essential office supplies. It also means being mindful of how resources are used and making sure that they are being used in the most efficient way possible.

Organizations must proactively find new ways to generate revenue to maximize profits. This could involve diversifying their product or service offerings, expanding into new markets, or finding new ways to reach existing customers. By having a solid financial management plan, organizations can identify areas where they can increase revenue and make informed decisions about allocating resources to achieve these goals.

Financial stability is another critical aspect of financial management. This means ensuring the organization has enough cash to cover expenses, including salaries, rent, utilities, and other costs. It also means having enough reserves to cover unexpected expenses or unexpected downturns in business. Organizations can achieve financial stability by generating enough revenue, managing costs effectively, and having a solid financial plan.

Risk management is also an essential part of financial management. Organizations must be aware of their risks and implement measures to mitigate them. This could involve having insurance to protect against losses, investing in security technology to protect sensitive information, or creating contingency plans in case of unforeseen events. By proactively managing risk, organizations can reduce the risk of financial loss and protect their bottom line.

A well-managed financial plan is essential for achieving growth and sustainability. By reducing expenses, maximizing profits, ensuring financial stability, and managing risk, organizations can make informed decisions about allocating resources and achieving their goals. With the help of sound financial management practices, organizations can achieve financial stability, reduce risk, and increase profits, ultimately helping them grow faster and more efficiently.

By adopting sound financial practices, organizations can achieve sustainable growth and reach new heights of success. By regularly reviewing financial statements and key performance indicators, organizations can identify areas where they need to make adjustments or improvements. This allows them to make informed decisions about allocating resources and changing their financial plan to achieve their goals more effectively.

Need to consider is the importance of financial transparency. Organizations should be open and honest about their financial situation with stakeholders and external stakeholders such as investors, customers, and suppliers.

This helps to build trust and credibility and can lead to better relationships and more opportunities for growth.

According to a study by the Small Business Administration, poor financial management is one of the primary reasons why small businesses fail. In addition, a lack of cash flow is the reason behind 82% of small business failures. This highlights the critical importance of financial management in ensuring the success and sustainability of a business.

Furthermore, a study by Deloitte found that companies with strong financial management practices are more likely to experience higher revenue growth and profitability levels. For example, the study found that companies with effective financial management practices had a median revenue growth rate of 21%, compared to just 7% for companies with poor financial management practices.

In addition, a report by McKinsey & Company found that companies that actively manage their working capital can achieve 30-40% higher returns on capital than companies that do not. This highlights the importance of effective financial management in maximizing profitability and returns on investment.

Overall, these data points demonstrate the critical role that financial management plays in the success and growth of an organization. Organizations must regularly review and adjust their financial plan to stay on track and adapt to changing circumstances. By visiting proactive and flexible, organizations can continue to achieve growth and sustainability over the long term.

Illustrating through practical examples

Founded in 2014, This new labs has experienced significant growth in recent years, with a client base that includes large corporations and startups in various industries. As a result, it has implemented several critical financial management practices to manage its finances effectively and support this growth.

One of the first steps this labs took was developing a well-designed financial management plan. This involved reviewing their financial situation, identifying potential growth and risk areas, and setting specific revenue and expense goals. By clearly understanding their financial situation, this labs could make informed decisions about allocating resources and prioritizing expenses.

This Labs also developed a forecasting process for their financial management plan. This involved analyzing past revenue and expenses, market trends, and other factors that could impact their business to predict future income and expenses. By having accurate forecasts, this labs could make informed decisions about future investments and expenditures and allocate resources more effectively.

Budgeting was another critical component of their' financial management plan. They created a detailed plan for their financial resources, including revenue and expenses, and allocated those resources to achieve specific goals. This allowed them to stay on track with their financial goals and maximize their resources.

In addition to these practices, it also focused on reducing expenses. They implemented automation in various areas of the organization, such as invoicing, accounting, and payroll. This reduced the workload of employees and the risk of human error, which can lead to financial loss. By being mindful of how resources are used and making sure that they are being used in the most efficient way possible, they were able to cut down on unnecessary costs.

To maximize profits, the company looked for new ways to generate revenue. This involved diversifying their service offerings, expanding into new markets, and finding new ways to reach existing customers. By having a solid financial management plan in place, they were able to identify areas where they could increase revenue and make informed decisions about how to allocate their resources to achieve these goals.

Financial stability was another critical aspect of the company's financial management practices. They ensured they had enough cash to cover their expenses, including salaries, rent, utilities, and other costs. They also had enough reserves to cover unexpected expenses or downturns in business. By managing its payments effectively and having a solid financial plan in place, This Labs achieved financial stability.

Risk management was also a priority for them. As a result, they were aware of their risks and implemented measures to mitigate them. This involved having insurance to protect against losses, investing in security technology to protect sensitive information, and creating contingency plans in case of unforeseen events. By being proactive about risk management, they were able to reduce the risk of financial loss and protect its bottom line.

Overall, the financial management practices implemented by this Labs have helped them to achieve sustainable growth and reach new heights of success. By reducing expenses, maximizing profits, ensuring financial stability, and managing risk, it has made informed decisions about allocating its resources and achieving its goals. As a result, with the help of sound financial management practices, it has achieved financial stability, reduced risk, and increased profits, ultimately helping them grow faster and more efficiently.

Take your time and try to answer these questions.

1) How did the company utilize financial management to drive growth and success in their business?

2) What financial management strategies did they implement to reduce expenses and increase revenue?

3) How did they balance the need for financial stability with the appetite for risk-taking in their business decisions?

4) What were some challenges they faced in implementing their financial management strategies, and how did they overcome them?

5) How did the company use automation and technology to improve their financial management practices, and what benefits did this bring to the company?

6) What lessons can other organizations learn from the financial management practices employed by them?

7) How can financial management be integrated into an organization's strategic planning process to maximize growth and sustainability?

8) How can organizations mitigate financial risks and ensure financial stability in an uncertain economic climate?

9) What are the long-term benefits of effective financial management, and how can these benefits be measured and tracked over time?

10) How can organizations ensure that financial management remains a priority as they continue to grow and scale their business?

How can it work for you?

Leadership teams can draw insights and lessons to inform their financial management strategies. Here are a few key takeaways that organizations can consider:

Develop a well-designed financial management plan: By having a clear understanding of their organization's economic situation, leaders can make informed decisions about how to allocate resources, prioritize expenses, and plan for future growth. This involves creating a plan for the organization's financial resources, including revenue and costs, and allocating those resources to achieve specific goals.

Forecast future revenue and expenses: Accurate forecasting allows organizations to make informed decisions about future investments and expenditures and allocate resources more effectively. Therefore, leaders should work to ensure that their forecasts are accurate and up-to-date.

Focus on reducing expenses: Implementing automation and cutting unnecessary costs can help organizations reduce expenses and increase profits. First, however, leaders should be mindful of how resources are used and make sure that they are being used in the most efficient way possible.

Be proactive about generating revenue: Organizations must find new ways to generate revenue. This could involve diversifying their product or service offerings, expanding into new markets, or finding new ways to reach existing customers.

Ensure financial stability: Financial stability means having enough cash to cover expenses, having enough reserves to cover unexpected costs or downturns in business, and generating enough revenue to ensure financial stability. Leaders should work to ensure that their organization is financially stable and has the resources necessary to weather any unexpected challenges.

Manage risk: Organizations must be aware of their risks and implement measures to mitigate them. This could involve having insurance to protect against losses, investing in security technology to protect sensitive information, or creating contingency plans in case of unforeseen events.

Organizations can use these insights to inform their financial management strategies and make informed decisions about allocating resources, prioritizing expenses, and planning for future growth. By taking a proactive approach to financial management, organizations can achieve financial stability, reduce risk, and increase profits, ultimately helping them grow faster and more efficiently.

Category	Evaluation	Strengths	Weakness	Actionable Steps
Budgeting				
Forecasting				
Negotiations				
Revenue Maximisation				
Expense Reduction				
Financial Stability				
Risk Management				

Organizations can use the above table to assess their current financial management practices, identify areas for improvement, and develop actionable steps to address any weaknesses or gaps in their financial management processes. By taking a proactive approach to financial management, organizations can ensure financial stability, reduce risk, and achieve sustainable growth.

Understanding how to manage cash flow, reduce expenses, and maximize profits is essential for financial stability. By following the insights and tips discussed in this article, you can evaluate your financial management practices and make informed decisions to drive growth in your organization. We encourage you to take action and implement these strategies to achieve financial stability and success.

Collaboration and Partnership for Growth

"Collaboration is the caffeine that fuels the engine of progress and growth, for it is only through partnership that we can brew a better future."

One of my clients is a leading B2B eCommerce company in Bengaluru, India, selling consumer durable and electronic products. The company had been operating for a few years and started in a 2BHK house in HSR Layout, Bengaluru. When I got associated with them, they had just moved to a cozy four-floor building that could accommodate around 120 people. The CEO was eager to take the company to the next level, and as part of my role, I advised him on the benefits of collaboration and partnerships for business growth.

After several months of strategic planning and market research, the company partnered with several other companies in the industry to expand its reach and access new customers. The CEO understood that partnering with other businesses in complementary sectors could provide a competitive edge and allow shared resources and cost savings.

One of the critical partnerships the company established was with a logistics provider with a strong presence in the region. The partnership allowed the company to offer customers faster delivery times and better logistics services, improving the overall customer experience. Additionally, the company collaborated with a leading market research firm to gain valuable insights into customer needs and preferences, enabling it to tailor its offerings better to meet customer demands.

Over time, these partnerships proved fruitful, and the company saw significant growth in its customer base and revenue. The CEO was thrilled with the progress and sought additional funding to accelerate the company's growth further.

The company eventually secured a series C investment of 100 million from a leading venture capital firm and expanded to a new building with more than 1000 employees. The investment was a testament to the company's success and demonstrated the power of collaboration and partnerships in achieving business growth.

With the additional funding, the company continued to pursue strategic partnerships and collaborations, expanding its reach and improving its competitiveness in the market. While the company faced challenges and setbacks, such as managing logistics and supply chain disruptions, it persevered and emerged stronger due to its commitment to collaboration and partnership.

The company's willingness to collaborate and partner with other organizations and its commitment to mutual success played a crucial role in its success. It demonstrated the power of strategic partnerships in achieving business growth.

Let's understand how collaboration and partnerships can help organizations reach new heights. From accessing new markets and customers to cost-efficiency and brand credibility, the benefits of collaboration are numerous and should not be overlooked.

Collaboration and partnerships are critical components of business success and growth. By forming strategic partnerships and collaborations with other organizations, companies can leverage the strengths of each partner to increase market reach, access new resources, and improve their competitiveness. This article will examine the key benefits of collaboration and partnerships for organizations and provide insights into how companies can effectively collaborate to achieve their goals.

One of the primary benefits of collaboration is the ability to access new markets and customers. By partnering with other organizations, companies can expand their reach beyond their traditional customer base and tap into new customer segments. For example, a company specializing in technology solutions might partner with a marketing firm to reach new customers in the technology sector. This partnership allows the technology company to leverage the marketing firm's expertise in customer engagement and brand building. In contrast, the marketing firm benefits from the technology company's technical knowledge and resources.

Collaboration is cost efficiency. By pooling resources and sharing costs, companies can reduce operating expenses and increase profitability. For example, two companies specializing in complementary products might jointly partner to produce a new product line. This partnership allows both companies to leverage their strengths and resources, reducing costs and increasing competitiveness.

Collaboration also presents opportunities for learning and skill development. Companies can learn from each other's best practices by working with other organizations and gaining new insights into their operations. This can help organizations identify new growth opportunities and improve their overall performance. For example, a company specializing in supply chain management might partner with a company specializing in logistics to enhance its delivery processes and reduce delivery times.

Partnerships and collaborations also help companies to sharpen their ability to handle challenges. Organizations can develop and implement effective solutions to complex business problems by pooling resources and working together. This can help companies stay ahead of the competition and improve their competitiveness. For example, two companies specializing in renewable energy might form a partnership to develop a new energy technology that combines their strengths and addresses a common challenge in the energy sector.

The vital benefit of collaboration and partnerships is the enhancement of brand credibility. By partnering with other organizations, companies can associate themselves with reputable and established brands, increasing their credibility and visibility in the market. This can help organizations attract new customers, improve their reputation, and increase their competitiveness.

In addition to these benefits, collaborations and partnerships can help organizations better understand their customers and the market. Companies can access valuable customer insights and market data by working with other organizations to inform their business strategies and decision-making. For example, a company specializing in financial services might partner with a market research firm to gain better insights into customer needs and preferences in the financial sector.

Companies must approach these relationships with clear goals and a shared vision to effectively collaborate and form successful partnerships. Establishing clear expectations and responsibilities for each partner and regularly communicating and assessing the partnership's progress is essential. Collaboration and affiliations should be built on trust and a shared commitment to mutual success.

Collaboration and partnerships can provide organizations with various benefits, including access to new markets and customers, cost-efficiency, learning, and skill development opportunities, a sharper ability to handle challenges, and enhanced brand credibility. However, to maximize the benefits of collaboration and partnerships, companies must approach these relationships with a clear strategy, a shared vision, and a commitment to mutual success.

These are some ingredients for thought on the power of collaboration and partnerships. Remember, the success of a business is not only determined by individual efforts but also by the strength of its partnerships.

Illustrating through practical examples

In the education industry, collaboration and partnerships can significantly improve student outcomes and the overall quality of education. One real-life example of successful cooperation in the education industry is the partnership between a leading educational materials and solutions provider and the University based in Arizona.

They are the leading provider of educational materials and solutions, while the University is a renowned public research university with a strong reputation for innovation and quality education. These two organizations formed a strategic partnership to develop new learning technologies and solutions that would help improve student outcomes and address the evolving needs of the education market.

The partnership focused on developing new digital tools and resources that could help students learn more effectively and engage more deeply with the learning process. The association also aimed to leverage the expertise of both organizations in data analytics and research to better understand student needs and preferences and inform the development of new educational solutions.

One of the key outcomes of the partnership was the development of the Provider Connect platform, which integrates digital tools, resources, and assessments into a single platform that can be customized to meet the unique needs of each student. In addition, the platform provides students access to interactive learning materials, personalized reviews, and real-time feedback, helping them learn more effectively and achieve better outcomes.

The partnership also led to developing the SmartBook adaptive learning platform, which uses data analytics and machine learning algorithms to create personalized learning paths for each student. The platform analyzes student performance data and adjusts the content and pace of learning to match the student's needs, providing a more personalized and engaging learning experience.

The collaboration between the provider and the University has also led to various research studies and initiatives to improve student outcomes and enhance the quality of education. For example, the two organizations have collaborated on an analysis of the impact of digital learning tools on student performance, which found that students who used the provider Connect platform achieved better grades and retention rates than those who did not.

The partnership between the provider and the University is a great example of how collaboration and partnerships can help organizations in the education industry improve student outcomes and enhance the quality of education. By leveraging the strengths of each partner and working together to develop new solutions, these organizations were able to create innovative digital tools and resources that have helped transform the students' learning experience. The partnership also provided valuable insights into student needs and preferences and contributed to the overall improvement of education in the United States.

Take your time and try to answer these questions.

1) What were the primary goals and objectives of the collaboration between the provider and the University, and how were they achieved?

2) What were the critical challenges faced by both organizations during the collaboration process, and how were they overcome?

3) How did the partnership between the provider and the University enhance the educational experience for students and teachers?

4) What were the key benefits and outcomes of the collaboration, both for the two organizations involved and for the broader education industry?

5) How did the collaboration change the education industry landscape, and what lessons can be learned from this case study for other organizations looking to collaborate in this space.

How can it work for you?

After reviewing the case study of the provider and the University, organizations can interpret the lessons learned from this successful collaboration in several ways. Here are a few key takeaways:

1) Focus on mutual goals: To succeed in a collaboration, it is essential to set clear and mutual goals from the outset. Both parties in the partnership should have a common goal focused on delivering value to end-users or customers. In this case, the collaboration between the provider and the University was driven by enhancing the educational experience for students and teachers.

2) Embrace innovation: Collaboration is an excellent opportunity to embrace innovation and explore new solutions to improve business operations or solve common industry problems. Organizations can leverage each other's strengths and expertise to develop new products, services, or systems they cannot create independently. In this case, the provider and the University collaborated and developed new educational solutions that improved the quality of education for students and teachers.

3) Prioritize open communication: Communication is critical to any successful collaboration. Organizations should prioritize available and regular contact with their partners to ensure everyone is on the same page and that any issues can be addressed quickly. In this case, both organizations provided regular communication to understand the challenges and opportunities of the partnership.

4) Manage risks effectively: Any partnership involves some level of risk, and it is essential to manage these risks effectively to ensure that the collaboration is successful. Organizations must work together to identify potential risks and create contingency plans to mitigate them. In this case, the provider and the University overcame some initial challenges by managing risks effectively.

5) Monitor and evaluate progress: It is crucial to monitor and assess the progress of the collaboration to ensure that it is on track and delivering the expected results. Organizations should regularly evaluate their progress

and make necessary adjustments to ensure the partnership remains successful. In this case, the provider and the University worked together to monitor progress, evaluate outcomes, and make necessary changes.

This case study highlights the value of collaboration and partnership for organizations. By embracing mutual goals, innovation, open communication, effective risk management, and regular evaluation, organizations can achieve success in their collaborations and achieve their goals.

Factor to Consider	Evaluation	Strengths	Weakness	Actionable Steps
Product/Service				
Customer Experience				
Marketing Strategy				
Sales Performance				
Operations				
Finance				
Human Resource				
Technology				
Legal/Regulatory				

First, use this table to identify the factors most relevant to your organization. For example, customer experience might be pivotal if you are a service-based company. Then, once you have identified the elements, list the strengths and weaknesses of your organization under each category.

For each strength or weakness, it is essential to provide specific examples and data to support your evaluation. For instance, if your power is in sales performance, provide metrics such as revenue growth or customer acquisition rates to support your assessment.

After completing the below table, use the information to create a summary report that identifies your organization's key strengths and weaknesses. Based on this analysis, identify actionable steps that can be taken to address weaknesses and leverage strengths to drive growth and success. This report can be used as a strategic planning and decision-making tool to help ensure that your organization focuses on the areas that will drive the most impact and success.

The benefits of collaboration and partnerships for organizations cannot be overstated. By leveraging the strengths of multiple organizations, companies can increase their market reach, access new resources, and improve their competitiveness. We encourage you to consider the benefits of collaboration and partnerships for your organization and to approach these relationships with a clear strategy, shared vision, and a commitment to mutual success. Take the first step towards collaboration and partnerships today and see how it can help your organization reach new heights.

Continuous Improvement for Growth

"Continuous improvement is the path to success. Embrace the journey, and never stop moving towards a better tomorrow."

It was a warm and bustling evening at the Hyatt, and I was there for a media event to present a paper on growth strategy. As I was sipping on a delicious piña colada, the Managing Director of an India-based media house approached me. We started chatting, and he shared his dream of improving his media house from the top 10 to no 1 in a visual medium. He was determined about what he would like to be in the next few years and wanted to collaborate on this exciting venture.

We both decided to work together on this project, and we started by encouraging collaboration and teamwork. We gathered a group of passionate and skilled individuals who were equally invested in this new venture. We brainstormed and shared our ideas and eventually devised a solid plan.

To ensure that our plan was effective, we conducted a thorough root cause analysis to identify the underlying causes of our challenges. As a result, we discovered that we needed to streamline our processes, adopt new technology, and focus on a customer-centric approach to achieve our goal.

We then focused on process standardization, which helped us to increase efficiency and consistency. Finally, we created a clear, concise strategy that was easy to follow and consistently applied.

As we progressed, we also focused on employee engagement. As a result, we created a positive working environment where everyone felt valued and motivated to contribute to the organization's success. In addition, we provided training and development opportunities that helped our employees to grow and develop new skills.

We also adopted technology to automate repetitive tasks and support our continuous improvement efforts. This helped us to streamline our processes, improve efficiency, and increase productivity.

To make informed decisions, we relied on data-driven decision-making. Analyzing data, we identified areas for improvement and made informed decisions that drove our success.

Throughout this two-year journey, we celebrated our successes and recognized our employees' efforts. This helped us to build new habits and reinforce the culture of continuous improvement.

Finally, our hard work paid off, and we launched not only one but two television channels. We were thrilled to have achieved our goal and taken our media house from print to visual medium. It was a proud moment for all of us, and we knew this was just the beginning.

Taking a media house from one of the top 10 to no 1 visual medium was filled with challenges and an exciting and fulfilling experience. By incorporating the core points of continuous improvement, we achieved our long-term goals and stayed ahead of the competition.

Continuous improvement is constantly analyzing and improving processes, products, and services to increase efficiency, reduce waste, and enhance customer experience. It involves a systematic approach to identify areas for improvement, implement best practices, and use data and analytics to measure progress and outcomes. This process is crucial for organizations that aim to stay ahead of the competition and achieve long-term success.

The continuous improvement process starts with defining a clear end goal for the organization. Next, this goal should be communicated to all employees, making them understand how their work contributes to the organization's success. This helps employees align their work with the organization's goals and create a sense of ownership and motivation.

The organization should have a clear framework for continuous improvement. This includes creating awareness programs and educating employees about the importance of continuous improvement and how it can help the organization grow. Organizations can also enhance communication by creating forums for employees to provide feedback, suggestions, and ideas for improvement. This helps create a continuous improvement culture where employees are encouraged to participate and contribute.

Organizations should also measure their outcomes regularly to determine the effectiveness of their continuous improvement efforts. This requires tracking key metrics such as customer satisfaction, process efficiency, and waste reduction. By periodically monitoring these metrics, organizations can identify areas for improvement and make necessary changes to achieve their end goal.

To ensure the success of continuous improvement, organizations must celebrate their successes. This helps to build new habits and reinforce the continuous improvement culture. Celebrating success also helps to recognize employees' efforts and boost their motivation.

- Collaboration: Encouraging collaboration and teamwork can help organizations to identify problems and find solutions more efficiently.

- Root cause analysis: Identifying the root cause of a problem is critical to finding an effective solution. Organizations should strive to understand the underlying causes of issues and work to eliminate them.

- Process standardization: Standardizing processes can increase efficiency and consistency. Organizations should create clear and concise, easy-to-follow, and consistently applied strategies.

- Employee engagement: Employee engagement is a critical component of continuous improvement. Organizations should strive to engage employees and create a positive working environment where employees feel valued and motivated to contribute to the organization's success.

- Technology adoption: Adopting technology can help organizations to streamline processes, improve efficiency, and increase productivity. Organizations should consider using technology to automate repetitive tasks and support continuous improvement efforts.

- Data-driven decision-making: Organizations should strive to make data-driven decisions. By analyzing data, organizations can identify areas for improvement and make informed decisions that will drive success.

- Customer-centric approach: Organizations should focus on delivering customer value and prioritizing their needs. This can be achieved by continuously improving processes and products to enhance the customer experience.

- Continuous learning: Organizations should encourage constant learning and professional development for employees. Organizations can help employees grow and develop new skills by providing training and development opportunities, contributing to the organization's success.

- Flexibility: Organizations should be flexible and adaptable to change. They should be able to respond quickly to changes in the market and adjust their strategies to remain competitive.

By incorporating these core points, organizations can create a culture of continuous improvement that drives success and growth.

Continuous improvement is crucial for organizations to stay ahead of the competition and achieve long-term success. Organizations can increase efficiency, reduce waste, and enhance the customer experience by continuously analyzing and improving processes, products, and services. Celebrating success and building a culture of continuous improvement is also essential to reinforce the process and create a positive working environment. Organizations can continuously improve and achieve their long-term goals by focusing on a clear end goal, having a clear framework, enhancing communication, and measuring outcomes regularly.

Illustrating through practical examples

One example of a company in the IT/ITES industry that has successfully implemented a continuous improvement process is a leading IT company in India. It is a global leader in consulting, technology, and outsourcing solutions, with over 250,000 employees in over 50 countries.

It has a clear end goal of delivering high-quality services and solutions to its clients while continuously improving its processes and enhancing the customer experience. To achieve this, it has implemented a comprehensive framework for continuous improvement, which includes the following key elements:

Collaboration: It encourages employee collaboration and teamwork to identify problems and find solutions more efficiently. It has established cross-functional teams that work together to identify and resolve issues, using various tools and techniques such as brainstorming, root cause analysis, and process mapping.

Root cause analysis: It strongly emphasizes identifying the root cause of problems to find practical solutions. It uses various analytical tools and techniques to understand the underlying causes of issues and works to eliminate them. For example, suppose a recurring problem exists with a particular process or system. In that case, it will investigate the root cause of the issue and work to resolve it rather than address the symptoms.

Process standardization: It has standardized its processes to increase efficiency and consistency. It has created clear and concise methods that are easy to follow and consistently applied across the organization. It also uses process mapping and improvement tools to continuously refine its processes and make them more efficient.

Employee engagement: It strongly emphasizes employee engagement, creating a positive working environment where employees feel valued and motivated to contribute to the organization's success. It offers a range of training and development opportunities to help employees grow and develop new skills, which can contribute to the organization's success.

Technology adoption: It has adopted various technologies to streamline processes, improve efficiency, and increase productivity. For example, it has developed a digital platform for its clients that uses advanced analytics and machine learning to deliver personalized solutions and services. It has also implemented robotic process automation (RPA) to automate repetitive tasks and reduce manual errors.

Data-driven decision-making: It uses data analytics to make informed decisions that drive success. It tracks key metrics such as customer satisfaction, process efficiency, and waste reduction to identify areas for improvement and measure the effectiveness of its continuous improvement efforts.

Customer-centric approach: It strongly focuses on delivering value to its customers and prioritizing their needs. It continuously improves its processes and products to enhance the customer experience and ensure that its solutions meet the evolving needs of its clients.

Continuous learning: It encourages constant learning and professional development for its employees. It offers a range of training and development opportunities to help employees grow and develop new skills, which can contribute to the organization's success.

Flexibility: It is flexible and adaptable to change, able to quickly respond to changes in the market and adjust its strategies to remain competitive. For example, during the COVID-19 pandemic, it quickly adapted to remote work and provided its employees with the necessary technology and tools to work from home.

Through its continuous improvement process, it has achieved significant success, improving its operations, reducing waste, and enhancing the customer experience. For example, it has achieved a 96% customer satisfaction rating and a 24% reduction in its carbon footprint. It has also won numerous awards for its commitment to continuous improvement, including the Deming Prize, the world's oldest and most prestigious award for total quality management.

It is an excellent example of an organization in the IT/ITES industry that has successfully implemented a continuous improvement process. By focusing on a clear end goal, having a clear framework, enhancing communication, and measuring outcomes regularly, it has been able to s growth and success over the years. We hope this case study has provided valuable insights into how continuous improvement can drive success in the IT/ITES industry. As you evaluate your organization, we encourage you to reflect on the core principles of continuous improvement and consider how to implement them in your processes. Remember to focus on collaboration, root cause analysis, process standardization, employee engagement, technology adoption, data-driven decision-making, customer-centric approach, continuous learning, and flexibility. Committing to continuous improvement, your organization can stay competitive, adapt to change, and achieve its long-term goals.

Take your time and try to answer these questions.

1) What are the key challenges that this Indian IT company faced, and how did they use the continuous improvement process to address them?

2) How did this Indian IT company create a culture of continuous improvement, and what steps did they take to involve employees in the process?

3) How did this Indian IT company measure the outcomes of its continuous improvement efforts, and what impact did these efforts have on the organization?

4) What role did collaboration and teamwork play in Its' success with continuous improvement?

5) How did they use data and analytics to inform its continuous improvement efforts, and what benefits did this provide?

6) How did this Indian IT company balance its customer-centric approach with the need to standardize processes and achieve greater efficiency?

7) How did they address the need for flexibility and adaptability in a rapidly changing market?

8) How did the company use technology to support its continuous improvement efforts, and what benefits did this provide?

9) How did this Indian IT company celebrate success and reinforce the organization's continuous improvement culture?

10) What lessons can be learned from their case study, and how can they be applied to our organization's continuous improvement efforts?

How can it work for you?

After reading and analyzing this Indian IT company's case study, organizations can interpret the fundamental principles of continuous improvement and apply them to their operations in several ways.

First, they can effectively define and communicate a clear end goal to all employees, ensuring everyone understands how their work contributes to the organization's success. This will help create a sense of ownership and motivation among employees and encourage them to align their work with the organization's goals.

Second, they can create a framework for continuous improvement, including education and awareness programs to help employees understand the importance of the process and how it can help the organization grow. They can also create forums for feedback and suggestions, encouraging employees to participate in the process and contribute their ideas for improvement.

Third, organizations can measure their outcomes regularly, tracking key metrics such as customer satisfaction, process efficiency, and waste reduction. By monitoring these metrics, organizations can identify areas for improvement and make necessary changes to achieve their end goal.

Fourth, organizations can celebrate successes, recognize employees' efforts, and reinforce the continuous improvement culture. This can help to build new habits and encourage employees to continue contributing to the organization's success.

In addition, organizations can adopt other fundamental principles of continuous improvement, such as collaboration and teamwork, root cause analysis, process standardization, employee engagement, technology adoption, data-driven decision-making, a customer-centric approach, continuous learning, and flexibility.

By incorporating these principles and practices, organizations can create a culture of continuous improvement that drives success and growth and ensures long-term sustainability in a rapidly changing market.

The table below is used to evaluate an organization's strengths, weaknesses, and actionable areas for improvement in continuous improvement.

The Growth Matrix

Aspects to Evaluate	Measurable Parameters	Strengths	Weakness	Evaluation
Customer Experience				
Process Efficiency				
Waste Reduction				
Employee Engagement				
Data-Driven Decision Making				
Continuous Learning				
Flexibility				

Based on the measurable parameters, identify the strengths and weaknesses of the organization in each aspect. Then, use the powers to build upon and address the shortcomings to improve organizational performance. Finally, continuously monitor progress and make necessary adjustments to achieve desired outcomes.

A continuous improvement is a fundamental approach for organizations to drive success and growth in the long term. Organizations can increase efficiency, reduce waste, and enhance the customer experience by implementing a systematic approach to identifying areas for improvement. As you move forward, remember the importance of measuring outcomes, celebrating successes, and encouraging a culture of collaboration, employee engagement, and continuous learning. Committing to continuous improvement, your organization can stay ahead of the competition and achieve long-term success.

Training and Development for Growth

"Viewing employee training and development as a strategic investment, rather than a mere cost, unlocks workforce potential and empowers them to drive organizational growth and excellence.."

I remember attending an industry conference in Dubai, where I had the opportunity to meet the Director of a prominent engineering organization. During our conversation, we discussed the critical role of employee training and development in the success of an organization. The Director expressed his concerns regarding the need for more training opportunities for their back-end staff, including the leadership team.

We discussed the various benefits of employee training and development, including improved job performance, increased employee satisfaction, and better leadership skills. I shared some examples of successful training programs I had implemented in other organizations, including personal and professional growth, improved communication skills, increased motivation, problem-solving skills, better time management, diversity and inclusion, and improved leadership skills.

The Director was interested in implementing similar training programs in their organization and asked me to help develop a customized training plan. I agreed to help and began by conducting a needs analysis to identify the specific training needs of their employees. We also identified the metrics to measure the success of the training program.

After the needs analysis, we developed a customized training plan that addressed their organization's specific needs. The project included classroom training, on-the-job training, mentorship, coaching, and e-learning. In addition, we had a variety of training methods to cater to the different learning styles of their employees.

To ensure the program's success, we included personal and professional growth, improved communication skills, increased motivation, problem-solving skills, better time management, diversity and inclusion, and improved leadership skills. We also emphasized the importance of continuous learning and development to keep pace with the changes in the industry.

We chose a group of employees to participate in a train-the-trainer program so that they could cascade the strategies down and continue the process. This helped to develop a pool of internal trainers who could deliver the training to other employees. The train-the-trainer program included developing their training skills, providing feedback, and coaching them to offer practical training.

The employees received the training program well, and the metrics significantly improved job performance, increased employee satisfaction, and better leadership skills. In addition, we received positive employee feedback, and many felt more valued and appreciated, contributing to higher employee morale and reduced turnover.

From personal and professional growth to work-related skill and knowledge growth programs, improved communication skills, increased motivation, and better leadership skills, we will explore the critical aspects of employee training and development and why it is crucial for the success of any organization.

Employee training and development play a vital role in the growth and success of an organization. Providing employees with opportunities to enhance their skills and knowledge through various training programs, mentorship, and educational chances improves job performance and increases employee satisfaction and retention. This, in turn, contributes to the overall success of the organization.

Organizations must adopt new methods and technologies to stay competitive in a constantly changing business environment. By investing in the professional development of their employees, organizations can keep pace with the changes in the industry and ensure their employees are equipped with the latest knowledge and skills. This helps deliver better quality products or services and gives the organization a competitive edge in the market.

Training and development for an organization can attract high-caliber talent. An organization that values the growth and development of its employees is more likely to attract top-level management and skilled workers. These employees are more likely to be motivated and engaged, which can lead to increased productivity.

Moreover, employee training and development can also increase job satisfaction and morale. Employees who feel that their organization values their professional growth and development are likelier to feel valued and appreciated. This increases job satisfaction, resulting in higher employee morale and reduced turnover.

Employee training and development can also lead to internal promotions, which can help organizations develop their existing talent and retain their employees. When employees see opportunities for growth within the organization, they are more likely to stay with the organization and contribute to its success. This saves the organization the time and resources required to find and train new employees and ensures a smooth transition of knowledge and experience.

Investing in employee training and development is investing in an organization's future growth and success.

- Personal and Professional Growth: Employee training and development programs can help employees grow personally and professionally. These programs provide employees with the skills and knowledge needed to excel in their current roles and prepare them for future organizational opportunities.

- Improved Communication Skills: Effective communication is essential for success in any organization. Employee training and development programs can help employees develop better communication skills, enhance teamwork, increase productivity, and foster a positive workplace culture.

- Increased Motivation: When employees feel that they are growing and developing professionally, they are more likely to be motivated and engaged in their work. This can increase job satisfaction, reduce turnover, and improve performance.

- Improved Problem-Solving Skills: Employee training and development programs can help employees develop critical thinking and problem-solving skills. These skills are essential for success in any role and can help employees find innovative solutions to challenges they face in the workplace.

- Better Time Management: Time management is crucial for any organization's success. Employee training and development programs can help employees develop better time management skills, increase productivity, reduce stress, and improve overall job performance.

- Diversity and Inclusion: Employee training and development programs can help organizations foster a diverse and inclusive workplace culture. These programs can give employees the knowledge and skills to understand and appreciate differences, increasing teamwork, productivity, and job satisfaction.

- Improved Leadership Skills: Employee training and development programs can help employees develop leadership skills essential for success in any role. These programs can help employees understand their leadership style, develop communication skills, and learn how to motivate and inspire others.

Employee training and development is an essential component of organizational growth and success. Organizations can improve job performance, increase employee satisfaction and morale, and attract high-caliber talent by providing employees with opportunities to enhance their skills and knowledge. In addition, investing in employees' professional development can give organizations a competitive edge in the market, increase internal promotions, and contribute to overall success.

Hence, organizations should prioritize employee training and development and allocate sufficient resources to support it. This can give employees the skills and knowledge they need to succeed in their current roles and prepare them for future opportunities. This investment will benefit the employees and lead to a more productive, efficient, and successful organization. Furthermore, by fostering a positive culture of continuous learning and development, organizations can ensure they have the skilled and knowledgeable workforce needed to meet the challenges of a rapidly changing business environment.

Illustrating through practical examples

One example of a media company that prioritizes employee training and development is the leading American media house. The Media house has been a leading news organization providing quality journalism for over a century. However, in recent years, the organization has recognized the need to invest in employee training and development to stay competitive in the rapidly changing media landscape.

The Media house offers a range of training and development programs for its employees. One such program is Digital Skills Training, a comprehensive program designed to help employees develop the digital skills needed to succeed in today's media industry. The program includes courses on social media, data analysis, and audience engagement.

Another program offered by the Media house is the Leadership Development Program. This program is designed for mid-level managers looking to develop their leadership skills and advance their careers. The program includes workshops, coaching sessions, and networking opportunities.

The Media house also offers a mentorship program for employees. The program pairs employees with mentors who can provide guidance and support as they navigate their careers within the organization. The program is designed to help employees develop new skills, gain new perspectives, and build relationships within the organization.

The results of the Media house's investment in employee training and development are impressive. The organization has attracted and retained top talent, and its employees are highly engaged and motivated. The organization has also stayed competitive in the rapidly changing media industry, thanks in part to the digital skills and leadership development programs offered to its employees.

One example of the success of the Media house's investment in employee training and development is the launch of its digital subscription service. The organization recognized the need to adapt to changing consumer behavior and launched a digital subscription service in 2011. The service's success can be attributed partly to the digital skills and audience engagement training provided to its employees.

The Media house is an example of a media organization that recognizes the importance of investing in employee training and development. By providing its employees with opportunities to enhance their skills and knowledge, the organization has been able to attract and retain top talent, stay competitive in the media industry, and achieve business success. Other media organizations looking to achieve similar success should consider investing in employee training and development as a critical component of their growth strategy.

Take your time and try to answer these questions.

1) What factors contributed to the media company's success in this case study?

2) How did the organization invest in employee training and development to achieve its goals?

3) What were the benefits of investing in employee training and development for the organization?

4) How did the organization measure the success of its employee training and development programs?

5) What challenges did the organization face in implementing its employee training and development programs, and how were these addressed?

6) How did the organization foster a culture of continuous learning and development among its employees?

7) What role did leadership play in the success of the organization's employee training and development programs?

8) How did the organization ensure its employee training and development programs aligned with its business strategy and goals?

9) What can other organizations learn from this case study to implement practical employee training and development programs?

10) How can the organization continue to build on its success in employee training and development to remain competitive?

How can it work for you?

After reviewing the case study of this Media house, the leadership team of an organization can interpret it and apply its critical learnings to their organization in several ways:

1) Assess their current training and development programs: The leadership team can evaluate their current employee training and development programs to identify areas that need improvement or expansion. They can also assess how their existing programs align with the needs of their employees and the organization.

2) Develop a comprehensive training and development strategy: Based on the identified gaps, the leadership team can develop an extensive training and development strategy that aligns with the organization's goals and objectives. This strategy should include clear learning

objectives, effective delivery methods, and relevant evaluation metrics.

3) Prioritize diversity and inclusion: The case study highlights the importance of diversity and inclusion in employee training and development. The leadership team can prioritize diversity and inclusion by integrating it into their training and development strategy and ensuring employees have the skills and knowledge to appreciate differences and work effectively with colleagues from diverse backgrounds.

4) Allocate sufficient resources: The leadership team must allocate financial and human resources to support the training and development strategy. This can include hiring additional staff or partnering with external training providers to deliver high-quality training programs.

5) Foster a culture of continuous learning: The case study emphasizes the importance of fostering a culture of constant learning in the organization. The leadership team can encourage continuous learning by promoting ongoing training and development opportunities, providing access to learning resources, and recognizing and rewarding employees who actively engage in learning and development.

By interpreting the key learnings from the case study and applying them to their organization, the leadership team can develop a practical employee training and development program that contributes to the overall growth and success of the organization.

Organizations can use this table to identify areas where they excel and need improvement. By measuring and tracking these metrics, they can develop a more actionable approach to employee training and development and create a plan for improving their weaknesses and capitalizing on their strengths. The summary report can include a detailed analysis of each aspect, a comparison with industry benchmarks, and actionable steps for improvement.

Aspects to Evaluate	Strengths	Weakness	Opportunities	Threats
Communication				
Motivation				
Problem-Solving Skills				
Time Management				
Diversity and Inclusion				
Leadership Skills				

Employee training and development is an essential investment for the growth and success of any organization. If you want to improve your company's productivity, attract high-caliber talent, and create a positive workplace culture, prioritize your employees' professional development. Please take the necessary steps to assess your organization's training and development needs and allocate sufficient resources to support them. By fostering a continuous learning and development culture, you can ensure that your workforce is equipped with the latest skills and knowledge needed to navigate the challenges of a rapidly changing business environment. So, consider investing in employee training and development programs today to secure your organization's future growth and success.

Data-Driven Decision for Growth

> *"Data-driven decision-making is the cornerstone of modern organizations, combining the power of technology, process, and culture to drive growth, success, and innovation."*

I had the opportunity to collaborate with a warehouse management and supply chain organization based in Jakarta, Indonesia, as a leadership coach and ISO compliance consultant. The organization had been grappling with a plateau in growth over an extended period, raising apprehensions among its stakeholders regarding their competitiveness in the market. In addition, although the organization had access to extensive data resources, it had yet to optimize them to drive growth or facilitate data-driven decision-making.

The first step in our engagement was to understand the vision and goals of the organization. Next, we worked closely with the executive team to identify their strategic priorities and determine the data sources needed to support these goals. We discovered that the organization had access to vast data, including customer feedback, sales data, and market trends. Still, they needed more infrastructure and tools to make sense of the data.

To address this, we developed a data management system that organized the data into a single data warehouse. We also created a suite of data visualization tools that enabled the executive team to quickly and easily access the data and gain insights into their operations.

Next, we conducted an in-depth data analysis to identify trends and patterns that informed decision-making. We utilized machine learning algorithms and statistical methods to extract meaningful insights from the data, including customer behavior patterns and operational inefficiencies.

Based on the insights gained from the data analysis, we developed a set of recommendations for the organization. These recommendations included changes to their product offerings, operational processes, and marketing strategy. We worked closely with the executive team to implement these changes and measure their impact on the organization's performance.

Over six months, the organization saw a significant improvement in its growth trajectory. They increased their customer base, reduced operational costs, and improved profitability. They were also able to project their growth to their investors, which resulted in a successful funding round from a top venture capital firm.

The organization was able to achieve these results by leveraging data-driven decision-making principles. By understanding their strategic priorities, organizing their data, and analyzing the data to gain insights, they could make informed decisions that drove growth and success. In addition, by investing in the right technology and developing a data-driven culture, the organization could sustain its development over the long term.

Data-Driven Decision for Growth

Data-driven decision-making has become an increasingly important aspect of modern organizations in today's digital age. Using data and analytics to inform decision-making and measure performance is crucial for driving growth and success in any industry. With the rise of technology and the growing abundance of data, businesses can now make more informed and evidence-based decisions to help them achieve their goals and stay ahead of the competition.

The first step in the data-driven decision-making process is to understand the vision and goals of the organization. This helps to ensure that the data collected and analyzed is relevant and aligned with the overall strategy. Once the vision and goals are clear, organizations can identify the data sources they need to access to make informed decisions. This can involve collecting data from various internal and external sources, such as sales data, customer feedback, and market trends.

The next step is to organize the data, which can be done through various methods such as data warehousing, data mining, and data visualization. This step is crucial as it helps to ensure that the data is easily accessible and can be used effectively to support decision-making.

Once the data is organized, the next step is to perform data analysis. This is where organizations can gain insights into the data and identify trends and patterns that inform decision-making. This can involve using statistical methods, machine learning algorithms, and other data analysis tools to extract meaningful insights from the data.

The final step in the data-driven decision-making process is to draw conclusions and make decisions based on the insights gained from the data analysis. This requires organizations to ask important questions such as: What do we already know about this data? What new information have we learned from this analysis? How can we use this information to meet our business goals?

By answering these questions, organizations can make informed and evidence-based decisions to help them achieve their goals and drive growth and success. In addition, data-driven decision-making can be applied to various business decisions, including how to drive profits and sales, establish good management behavior, optimize operations, and improve team performance.

It is also essential for organizations to have the right technology and data infrastructure to support their data-driven initiatives. This includes having robust data management systems, reliable data storage solutions, and secure data networks. In addition, organizations should also invest in data-driven tools and technologies that can help them collect, organize, and analyze data efficiently and effectively.

Moreover, organizations must have a data-driven culture where data is valued and integrated into every aspect of decision-making. This involves empowering employees with the right data skills and training them to use data to inform decision-making. Encouraging a data-driven culture also consists in making data accessible to everyone in the organization and creating a supportive environment where employees are encouraged to use data to drive innovation and decision-making.

Another critical aspect of data-driven decision-making is data governance. This involves establishing processes and policies for collecting, storing, and using data responsibly and ethically. This includes ensuring data is accurate, secure, and compliant with privacy regulations and industry standards.

Data-driven decision-making has become an essential aspect of modern organizations. With the right tools and techniques, businesses can use data and analytics to inform their decision-making and measure performance, which can drive growth and success. Success requires a combination of technology, process, and culture. By leveraging data and analytics, organizations can make informed, evidence-based decisions that drive growth and success and stay ahead in today's competitive marketplace. Organizations can make informed, evidence-based decisions that drive growth and success by leveraging data and analytics.

Illustrating through practical examples

The SaaS industry has been a leader in leveraging data-driven decision-making to drive growth and success. As a result, many companies implement data-driven processes, and this American SaaS company is one among them. It is a leading provider of inbound marketing and sales software. The company aims to help businesses grow by attracting, engaging, and delighting customers. To achieve this vision, it has implemented a robust data-driven decision-making process.

The first step in it's process is understanding the company's vision and goals. It's vision is to transform how businesses grow by delivering a powerful and easy-to-use platform that enables businesses to attract, engage, and delight customers. The company has set several goals to achieve this vision, including increasing customer acquisition, improving customer retention, and driving revenue growth.

The next step is identifying the data sources it needs to access to make informed decisions. It collects data from various sources, including customer feedback, marketing analytics, and sales data. The company also tracks customer behavior on its platform, which helps it understand how customers use its products and services.

Once the data is collected, it organizes it using data warehousing and data visualization techniques. This helps ensure the data is easily accessible and can be used effectively to support decision-making.

It then analyses data to gain insights into the data and identify trends and patterns that can inform decision-making. The company uses various data analysis tools, including statistical methods and machine learning algorithms, to extract meaningful insights from the data.

The final step is to draw conclusions and make decisions based on the insights gained from the data analysis. It uses these insights to inform its marketing, sales, and product development strategies. For example, the company may use customer feedback data to identify areas for improvement in its products or use marketing analytics data to optimize its marketing campaigns.

It's data-driven decision-making process has helped the company achieve its business goals. For example, the company has increased customer acquisition by 50% and improved customer retention by 30%. It has also been able to drive revenue growth by 40%.

It has invested in technology and data infrastructure to support its data-driven initiatives. As a result, the company has a robust data management system, reliable data storage solutions, and secure data networks. It has also invested in data-driven tools and technologies that help it collect, organize, and analyze data efficiently and effectively.

It has also created a data-driven culture where data is valued and integrated into every aspect of decision-making. The company empowers its employees with the right data skills and trains them to use data to inform their decision-making. It also makes data accessible to everyone in the organization and creates a supportive environment where employees are encouraged to use data to drive innovation and decision-making.

In conclusion, It's success in leveraging data-driven decision-making to drive growth and success is a testament to the power of this process in the SaaS industry. By following a similar approach and investing in technology, data infrastructure, and data-driven culture, other SaaS companies can achieve their business goals and stay ahead in today's competitive marketplace.

Take your time and try to answer these questions.

1) How did it's data-driven approach contribute to the company's success?

2) Can you identify examples of how it used data to make informed decisions and drive growth?

3) How did it's culture support and enable its data-driven decision-making?

4) What data management and analysis tools and technologies did it use to support its data-driven initiatives?

5) How did it ensure data accuracy, security, and compliance with privacy regulations and industry standards?

6) How did it use data to optimize its operations and improve team performance?

7) How did it's leadership team integrate data into their decision-making processes?

8) Can you identify any potential challenges or risks associated with a data-driven approach to decision-making? How did it address these challenges?

9) How other organizations in the SAAS industry, can learn from it's data-driven approach and apply it to their own business?

How can it work for you?

Organizations in the SAAS industry can learn a lot from it's data-driven approach and apply it to their own business. Here are some ways that organizations can interpret the case study and use it in their organization:

1) Identify your organization's vision and goals: To start, it's essential to understand your vision and goals clearly.

This will help ensure that the data you collect and analyze is relevant and aligned with your overall strategy.

2) Collect and analyze relevant data: Organizations should identify the data sources they need to access to make informed decisions. This can involve collecting data from various internal and external sources, such as sales data, customer feedback, and market trends. Once the data is collected, it should be organized, analyzed, and interpreted to gain insights into trends and patterns that inform decision-making.

3) Invest in data-driven tools and technologies: To support data-driven initiatives, organizations should invest in data-driven tools and technologies that can help them collect, organize, and analyze data efficiently and effectively. This includes having robust data management systems, reliable data storage solutions, and secure data networks.

4) Build a data-driven culture: It's essential to build a data-driven culture where data is valued and integrated into every aspect of decision-making. This involves empowering employees with the right data skills and training them to use data to inform decision-making. Encouraging a data-driven culture also consists in making data accessible to everyone in the organization and creating a supportive environment where employees are encouraged to use data to drive innovation and decision-making.

5) Establish data governance policies: Organizations should establish processes and procedures for collecting,

storing and using data responsibly and ethically. This includes ensuring data is accurate, secure and compliant with privacy regulations and industry standards.

Apply it's data-driven approach to their own business by identifying their vision and goals, collecting and analyzing relevant data, investing in data-driven tools and technologies, building a data-driven culture, and establishing data governance policies. By doing so, organizations can make informed, evidence-based decisions that drive growth and success and stay ahead in today's competitive marketplace.

Strengths	Weakness

Readers can use this table as a starting point to evaluate and find strengths and weaknesses in their organization. For example, they can assess their organization's strengths in solid data management, robust data infrastructure, access to various data sources, well-established data governance, supportive leadership for data-driven decision-making, and effective use of data.

They can also identify areas of weakness such as a lack of data-driven culture, limited data analysis skills, inefficient data analysis process, limited investment in data-driven tools and technologies, lack of clarity on organizational goals and vision, inconsistent data quality, inability to integrate data across departments, and inadequate data security measures.

Once strengths and weaknesses are identified, readers can create a measurable and actionable plan to address these areas. For example, suppose an organization's weakness is a need for data-driven culture. In that case, they can take actionable steps to encourage a culture that values data and integrates it into decision-making. This can include regular training and upskilling of employees in data analysis, making data accessible to everyone in the organization, and creating a supportive environment where employees are encouraged to use data to drive innovation and decision-making.

Overall, by using this table to evaluate and find strengths and weaknesses in their organization, readers can develop a plan to leverage data and analytics to inform decision-making, which can drive growth and success in today's competitive marketplace.

By leveraging data and analytics, organizations can make informed, evidence-based decisions that drive growth and success and stay ahead in today's competitive marketplace. We hope this article has provided valuable insights and practical steps that you can take to implement a data-driven approach in your organization.

We encourage you to explore additional resources and seek expert guidance to help you develop and implement a successful data-driven strategy. With the right tools, technology, and culture, you can unlock the full potential of data and analytics to drive growth, innovation, and success in your organization.

The Growth Matrix

Sustainable Business Practice for Growth

"Sustainability involves balancing customer satisfaction, strategic growth, and environmental responsibility to achieve long-term success for the business and the community, creating a better future for all."

Tiruppur, a small town in India, significantly contributes to the Indian garment industry, particularly knitwear, accounting for about 45 percent of India's total output. The Tamilnadu center of Tirupur is instrumental in this sector, generating up to 80 percent of knitted garment exports, which translates to approximately 4 percent of India's overall export trade. I collaborate closely with leading knitting export companies that distribute products to the United States and Spain. Despite intense competition, these companies face pressure to lower prices while maintaining product quality.

During a meeting with the leadership team, various options were presented for mitigating the pressure to reduce prices without compromising quality. As a participant, I introduced the concept of sustainable business practices, inspired by the Australian government's promotion of sustainable business opportunities and the increasing awareness of environmental issues. This idea sparked enthusiasm among the team as it offered the potential to reduce the company's impact on the environment and attract customers who valued ethical and environmentally conscious products.

Our approach to building a sustainable business model started with a focus on delivering value to our customers. To achieve this, we conducted an in-depth analysis of our customer's needs and preferences. Then we developed a sustainable business model that met those needs while reducing waste and minimizing environmental harm.

One of our first steps was to source materials from sustainable and ethical sources, such as organic cotton, recycled polyester, and natural dyes. These materials meet our high-quality environmental standards, allowing us to deliver environmentally friendly and appealing products to our customers.

Customer satisfaction and geographical footprint were also a priority for us. By balancing the growth of the business with a commitment to sustainability, we created a loyal customer base that appreciated the brand's values and ethical practices.

The company used zero-waste design techniques, ensuring that every piece of fabric was used and there was no waste. Additionally, all the clothing was designed to be long-lasting, minimizing the need for customers to replace their clothing frequently.

We took a proactive approach to educate our customers about sustainability. For example, our ad campaign featured highlighting the environmental benefits of their products, and they also produced educational materials that explained the importance of sustainability in the fashion industry.

We started communicating the company's sustainability goals to employees, customers, and other stakeholders, creating a shared sense of purpose and a commitment to sustainability. This ensured everyone worked towards the same goal and contributed to the business's success.

The company's employees were an essential part of its sustainability efforts. They were fully onboard with the company's sustainability goals, and the company ensured they understood their role in achieving them.

We also created a platform open to new ideas and encouraged the employees to come forward with suggestions for improving their sustainability practices. As a result, it fostered a culture of innovation and was always looking for ways to enhance its sustainability efforts.

Companies are pressured to adopt sustainable practices that reduce waste, minimize environmental harm, and enhance their reputation in today's business landscape. While growth is an important goal for any business, it should not come at the expense of environmental responsibility and customer satisfaction. Let's explore the key elements companies can implement to achieve sustainable, long-term growth.

Sustainable business practices are essential for companies looking to reduce waste, minimize environmental harm, and enhance their reputation. By adopting environmentally and socially responsible business strategies, organizations can build a positive image and attract customers and employees who share their values. In turn, this helps ensure long-term success for the company. To achieve sustainable business practices, companies should focus on the following key elements:

Value Delivery

Companies must understand the value they deliver to their customers and ensure that their business practices align with this value. Companies must better understand their customers' needs and create a sustainable business model that meets them while reducing waste and minimizing environmental harm.

Customer Satisfaction and Geographical Footprint

Companies should prioritize both delivering excellent customer service and expanding their geographical footprint. This involves effectively managing cash flow, margins, and investment to enter new markets and drive growth. Companies can ensure long-term success and achieve sustainable development by focusing on customer satisfaction and strategically expanding their geographical footprint. It is essential to balance growing the business and maintaining a positive reputation by delivering value to customers while being mindful of their impact on the surrounding communities and environment.

Customer Centricity

Companies should always keep their customers at the forefront of their minds and tailor their business practices accordingly. This means considering the impact of their products and services on the environment and ensuring that they are providing value to their customers while reducing waste and minimizing harm to the environment.

Educate Customers

Companies should educate their customers about the importance of sustainability and their role in reducing waste and minimizing environmental harm. Achieve it through educational materials, in-store displays, and other marketing efforts.

Clear Articulation of Goals

Companies should communicate their sustainability goals to employees, customers, and other stakeholders. Create a shared sense of purpose and ensure everyone works towards the same goal.

An Outside-In Look

Companies should take an outside-in approach to their business practices, considering the impact of their products and services on the environment and the communities in which they operate, which helps manage sustainably and meets the needs of their customers and communities.

Earn the Team

Companies must ensure that their employees are entirely on board with their sustainability goals and clearly understand their role in achieving them: effective communication, training, and a strong commitment from senior management.

Open for New Ideas

Companies should always be open to new ideas and encourage employees to come forward with suggestions for improving their sustainability practices. Foster a culture of innovation and ensure that companies always look for ways to enhance their sustainability efforts.

Take Ownership

Companies should take ownership of their sustainability practices and be willing to take the necessary steps to ensure they operate sustainably. This means making the required investments in technology, processes, and training and being willing to adapt and change as circumstances dictate.

Spread Knowledge

Companies should share their sustainability knowledge and best practices with other companies and organizations to help drive the adoption of sustainable business practices. Create a network of companies and organizations working towards a common goal and helps to build a more sustainable future for everyone.

Consistency

Companies should maintain consistency in their sustainability efforts and stay consistent with their goals. Ensure that companies operate sustainably over the long term and that their actions positively impact the environment.

People and Purpose Connection

Companies should connect their sustainability efforts to their sense of purpose and ensure their employees understand why their work is essential. Create a strong sense of purpose and a shared commitment to sustainability, which is necessary for long-term success.

Companies that adopt sustainable business practices can benefit significantly in terms of reputation and long-term success. Companies can ensure they operate sustainably and reduce waste and environmental harm by focusing on value delivery, customer satisfaction, and clearly articulating goals. Additionally, by educating customers and encouraging team buy-in, companies can foster a culture of sustainability and ensure that their efforts positively impact the environment and the communities in which they operate. Companies must also be open to new ideas, take ownership of their sustainability practices, and maintain consistency in their efforts to achieve long-term success. Finally, the connection of people and purpose is also critical, as it helps to create a strong sense of purpose and a shared commitment to sustainability among employees. By incorporating these key elements, companies can achieve sustainable, long-term growth and play an essential role in creating a more sustainable future for everyone.

By balancing customer satisfaction, strategic growth, and environmental responsibility, companies can achieve sustainable development and play an essential role in creating a better future for all. In addition, by prioritizing sustainability, companies can achieve financial success and positively impact the world.

Illustrating through practical examples

This small Spanish apparel company is a company that has become synonymous with sustainability and environmental responsibility in the outdoor apparel industry. Founded in 1973, it has always been committed to reducing waste, minimizing environmental harm, and creating high-quality outdoor apparel that meets the needs of its customers. Over the years, it has implemented several sustainable business practices that have helped the company achieve long-term growth and success.

Value Delivery: It understands its customers value high-quality outdoor apparel designed to last. As such, the company has focused on creating durable, long-lasting products made with sustainable materials and processes. For example, it has developed its line of organic cotton grown without harmful pesticides and fertilizers. The company also uses recycled materials in many products, such as recycled polyester.

Customer Satisfaction and Geographical Footprint: It has prioritized customer satisfaction and strategic growth in its business model. The company has expanded its geographical footprint by opening new stores in key markets worldwide, such as Tokyo and London. Additionally, it has invested in digital marketing and e-commerce, which has allowed the company to reach customers in new markets and increase sales.

Customer Centricity: It has always put its customers first and has tailored its business practices accordingly. The company's products are designed with the needs of its customers in mind while also considering the environmental impact. For example, it's fleece products are made from recycled plastic bottles, reducing waste and minimizing the company's carbon footprint.

Educate Customers: It has been a leader in educating its customers about the importance of sustainability and environmental responsibility. The company's website features several educational materials, such as videos and articles, that explain the impact of its products on the environment and the steps it takes to reduce that impact.

Clear Articulation of Goals: It has communicated its sustainability goals to its employees, customers, and other stakeholders. The company's mission statement, which includes a commitment to environmental responsibility, is prominently displayed on its website and stores. Additionally, it has set ambitious sustainability goals, such as becoming carbon neutral by 2025.

An Outside-In Look: It takes an outside-in approach to its business practices, considering the impact of its products and services on the environment and the communities in which it operates. The company has a team of sustainability experts responsible for evaluating its products' environmental impact and developing strategies to reduce that impact.

Earn the Team: It ensures that its employees are entirely on board with its sustainability goals and clearly understand their role in achieving them. In addition, the company offers training and education programs to help employees understand the importance of sustainability and their role in reducing waste and minimizing environmental harm.

Open for New Ideas: It is always open to new ideas and encourages its employees to come forward with suggestions for how the company can improve its sustainability practices. As a result, the company has implemented several innovative sustainability initiatives, such as a program that allows customers to return used its products for recycling.

Take Ownership: It takes ownership of its sustainability practices and is willing to take the necessary steps to ensure that it operates sustainably. The company has made significant investments in sustainable technology and processes, such as a solar-powered distribution center and a program to reduce water usage in its supply chain.

Spread Knowledge: It shares its sustainability knowledge and best practices with other companies and organizations in the outdoor apparel industry. The company has partnered with other companies to develop sustainable materials and processes and has shared its sustainability expertise through speaking engagements, conferences, and published materials.

One notable example is it's partnership with a Swiss tech company developing sustainable textile finishing technologies. Through this partnership, it and Beyond Surface Technologies developed a new water-repellent treatment free from harmful chemicals and more environmentally friendly than traditional treatments.

This partnership benefited it and the broader outdoor apparel industry, as other companies looking to improve their sustainability practices can use the new treatment.

Consistency: It is known for its character in sustainability efforts. The company has maintained its commitment to sustainability since its inception in 1973. The company's mission statement is "Build the best product, cause no unnecessary harm, use business to inspire and implement solutions to the environmental crisis." This statement is a clear reflection of the company's commitment to sustainability, and it is reinforced through its actions.

People and Purpose Connection: The company has also connected its sustainability efforts to its sense of purpose. It's employees understand the importance of sustainability and its connection to its mission.

The company provides training and education programs to its employees to ensure they know their sustainability goals and their role in achieving them. It also encourages its employees to live sustainable lifestyles by providing incentives to reduce their environmental impacts, such as public transportation subsidies and free bike repair services.

Take your time and try to answer these questions.

Here are a few critical detailed questions that could be asked to a leadership team of your organization that has gone through the its case study:

1) What were some of the key sustainability initiatives that it implemented? How did these initiatives align with the company's overall mission and values?

2) How did It's sustainability efforts impact the company's bottom line? Were there any financial benefits to pursuing a sustainable business model?

3) What challenges did it face in implementing sustainable practices, and how did the company overcome them?

4) How did it communicate its sustainability initiatives to customers, employees, and other stakeholders? Were there any particularly effective communication strategies that the company used?

5) In your opinion, what are some of the key takeaways that other organizations can learn from it's sustainability efforts? How could these insights be applied in your own company?

How can it work for you?

If an organization is looking to interpret the case study of this Spanish apparel company and apply it to its sustainability efforts, here are some key takeaways and steps they can consider:

1) Identify areas for improvement: Review the company's sustainability practices and identify areas needing improvement. This could include reducing waste, sourcing more sustainable materials, or decreasing energy consumption.

2) Set clear and ambitious goals: The organization should set clear and ambitious plans for sustainability. These goals should be aligned with the company's values and purpose.

3) Involve employees: Engage employees in the company's sustainability efforts. Please encourage them to share their ideas and suggestions and provide training to help them understand the importance of sustainability.

4) Build partnerships: Collaborate with other organizations, suppliers, and stakeholders to build sustainable partnerships. This could include working with suppliers to source more sustainable materials or partnering with other organizations to support environmental initiatives.

5) Communicate transparently: It's transparent communication about its sustainability efforts has been critical in building customer trust. Organizations should communicate their sustainability initiatives transparently and regularly internally and externally.

6) Continuously improve: Sustainability is an ongoing process and requires continuous improvement. Therefore, organizations should regularly review their sustainability practices, measure their progress toward goals, and identify areas for further improvement.

Organizations seeking to apply it's sustainability practices should identify areas for improvement, set clear goals, involve employees, build partnerships, communicate transparently, and continuously improve.

Reviewing current practices can help identify areas that require improvement, such as reducing waste and sourcing sustainable materials. Goals should be clear and ambitious, aligned with the organization's values and purpose. Engage employees by providing training and encouraging their ideas.

Build partnerships with suppliers and stakeholders to support environmental initiatives. Communicate sustainability efforts transparently and regularly to build trust. Sustainability is an ongoing process, so organizations should regularly review practices, measure progress, and identify areas for improvement.

By following these steps, organizations can interpret the lessons from it's sustainability efforts and apply them to their practices, helping them achieve their sustainability goals and positively impact the environment.

Category	Evaluation Criteria	Strengths	Weakness	Possibles	Threats
Environmental Impact	Energy Consumption				
	Waste Management				
	Water Management				
Social Impact	Employee Engagement				
	Diversity & Inclusion				
	Community Involvement				
Economic Impact	Financial Performance				

Here's a table to help readers evaluate their organization's strengths, weaknesses, opportunities, and threats to sustainability:

The action items column provides actionable steps organizations can take to address their weaknesses and take advantage of opportunities. It's important to regularly evaluate and update this table to ensure that sustainability efforts continuously improve and align with organizational goals.

It is an excellent example of a company that has successfully integrated sustainability into its business operations and positively impacted the environment. As you evaluate your organization's sustainability efforts, consider implementing some of the best practices highlighted in this case study.

Identify areas where your organization can improve and take action towards positively impacting the environment. Let us all do our part in creating a more sustainable future.

Global Expansion for Growth

"Broadening your reach beyond borders unveils endless opportunities for expansion and prosperity."

I had the opportunity to work with a highly successful electronics manufacturer in the United States. Despite being a top contender in their domestic market, the company experienced a slowdown in growth due to increased competition. As a result, the decision was made to explore global expansion to enhance its competitive position and expand its market reach.

Extensive market research was conducted, and India was identified as a strategic target due to its significant population and rapidly growing economy. As a result, the company established new manufacturing plants and distribution centers in India and hired local employees with specialized skills and expertise to maximize cost savings and access a larger talent pool.

The global expansion initiative proved fruitful, as the company experienced significant growth in revenue and profitability, and the brand's recognition expanded in the Asian market. Furthermore, the company reduced its reliance on the US market and diversified its market share.

Despite the many advantages of international expansion, there were obstacles to overcome. The company had to adapt its products and business practices to suit the local market and comply with local regulations. For example, the company had to modify its products to meet local safety standards and obtain the required certifications.

The expansion into India enabled the company to capitalize on new opportunities and markets, thereby increasing its competitive edge and business growth. This success exemplifies the value of global expansion as a viable business strategy, even in the face of cultural and regulatory challenges.

It is a topic of global expansion, a strategy that many organizations use to increase their reach and competitiveness in the worldwide market. We'll examine the benefits and challenges of expanding operations into international markets and discuss how companies can grow bigger and better by tapping into new opportunities and markets.

Global expansion refers to expanding a company's operations into international markets to increase its market reach, access new customers, and reduce dependence on its domestic market. By expanding globally, organizations can access new markets, increase revenue, and improve their competitive position. The benefits of global expansion are numerous and diverse and can help organizations grow bigger and better.

Greater Reach: By establishing a presence in an international market, organizations can reach more customers and potential clients. This expands the customer base and provides new growth and revenue generation opportunities. As a result, companies can increase their market share and reach more customers, leading to higher sales and increased profitability.

Improved Access to Talent: Global expansion allows companies to access a larger talent pool and expertise. Companies can hire employees from different countries who bring with them diverse skills, experiences, and perspectives. This can increase innovation, creativity, and problem-solving skills, improving a company's competitiveness.

Access to New Facilities: Global expansion provides companies with new and improved facilities in different countries. For example, companies can build new manufacturing plants, distribution centers, and research facilities, which can help them to increase production and efficiency, reduce costs, and improve the quality of their products.

Diversifying Company Markets: Global expansion allows companies to diversify their markets and reduce dependence on a single call. In addition, by operating in multiple countries, companies can spread their risks and mitigate the impact of economic downturns or other factors that may negatively impact one market. This can provide companies with more excellent stability and security over the long term.

Greater Brand Awareness: Expanding globally can also increase a company's brand awareness and recognition. By operating in multiple countries, companies can reach new customers who may not be familiar with their brand. This can increase brand exposure and help companies establish a more substantial reputation and presence in the global market.

Investment Opportunities: Global expansion can also provide companies with investment opportunities, such as new projects, joint ventures, and acquisitions. By investing in international markets, companies can tap into new sources of capital, which can help them to grow their business and increase their competitiveness.

Cultural Differences: While expanding globally can provide many benefits, it also presents many challenges, including cultural differences. Companies must be sensitive to local cultural norms, traditions, and values and must be prepared to adapt their products, services, and business practices to meet the needs of local customers.

Compliance and Regulatory Issues: Companies must also be aware of and compliant with local laws and regulations when expanding globally. This includes ensuring compliance with labor laws, taxes, and environmental regulations, among other things. Companies that fail to comply with local laws and regulations can face significant financial and reputational consequences.

The global expansion provides companies with many benefits and opportunities to grow bigger and better. By expanding into international markets, companies can access new customers, increase revenue, and improve their competitive position.

However, companies must be aware of and prepared for the challenges of global expansion, including cultural differences and compliance and regulatory issues. Overall, international expansion is a valuable strategy for organizations looking to grow their business and increase their competitiveness in the global market.

Global expansion is a powerful tool for organizations looking to increase their market reach, access new customers, and improve their competitiveness in the worldwide market. By understanding the benefits and challenges of international expansion, companies can make informed decisions about expanding their operations and making the most of new opportunities for growth and success.

Illustrating through practical examples

One real-life example of a startup company that has successfully expanded globally is a online market place homestay. Founded in 2008, they started as a small home-sharing platform in San Francisco but quickly expanded its operations to become a global leader in the hospitality industry.

One of the critical benefits of it's global expansion was the ability to access new markets and reach more customers. By expanding into different countries, it could tap into new customer segments interested in unique travel experiences and alternative accommodations. This expanded it's customer base and provided new growth and revenue generation opportunities.

Another benefit of it's global expansion was improved access to talent. It was able to hire employees from different countries who brought with them diverse skills, experiences, and perspectives. This increased innovation, creativity, and problem-solving skills improving it's overall competitiveness.

To ensure success in its global expansion, it was sensitive to cultural differences and adapted its products and services to meet the needs of local customers.

For example, in Japan, it partnered with local hosts to provide traditional Japanese experiences such as tea ceremonies and sushi-making classes, which appealed to Japanese customers and helped them to establish a more substantial reputation there.

It also faced compliance and regulatory issues when expanding globally, particularly in markets where home-sharing was not yet regulated. To address these issues, it worked with local governments to establish regulations allowing for safe and responsible home-sharing while protecting local communities.

It operates in over 220 countries today, with over 4 million listings on its platform. Its global expansion has allowed the company to diversify its markets and reduce its dependence on a single market, providing more excellent stability and security over the long term. It has also increased It's brand awareness and recognition, establishing the company as a leader in the hospitality industry worldwide.

It's success in global expansion serves as an example of the benefits and challenges that come with expanding operations into international markets. By understanding the importance of cultural sensitivity, compliance and regulatory issues, and diversifying markets, startup companies can follow in it's footsteps and succeed in the global market.

Take your time and try to answer these questions.

Here are some critical detailed questions that could be asked to a leadership team of an organization who go through the case study on this online market place homestay:

1) What do you think are the key factors that contributed to it's success in the global market?

2) How did it overcome the challenges of cultural differences and regulatory issues when expanding globally?

3) How did it leverage technology to enhance its business model and improve its competitiveness?

4) What strategies did they employ to differentiate itself from its competitors and gain market share?

5) How did it's business model evolve, and how did these changes affect its success?

6) What lessons can other companies learn from it's global expansion and innovation approach?

7) What were their's most significant risks during its growth, and how did the company manage them?

8) How did it establish and maintain its brand identity across different markets and cultures?

9) What role did leadership and organizational culture play in it's success, and how can other companies replicate this?

10) What challenges do you think it will face as it continues to expand its operations and explore new markets?

How can it work for you?

After analyzing the case study on it and answering the critical questions related to the company's success in global expansion, an organization's leadership team can interpret the findings in several ways. Here are a few examples:

1) Identifying opportunities for global expansion: Based on ' success story, the leadership team can assess whether their organization can expand globally and tap into new markets. In addition, they can analyze the similarities and differences between their organization and it regarding business models, product/service offerings, customer base, and other factors to identify potential opportunities for global expansion.

2) Evaluating risks and challenges: The leadership team can learn from it's challenges and risks during its global expansion journey. They can assess whether their organization can handle cultural differences, regulatory issues, and other challenges of expanding into international markets. Understanding the risks and challenges, they can develop a plan to mitigate them and ensure a smooth transition into new markets.

3) Innovating through technology: Another critical learning from its case study is the importance of leveraging technology to enhance the business model and improve competitiveness. The leadership team can analyze how their organization can incorporate technology into their operations to enhance efficiency, improve customer experience, and gain a competitive edge.

4) Developing a strong brand identity: It's approach to establishing and maintaining a solid brand identity can also be a valuable lesson for other organizations. The leadership team can evaluate its brand identity and determine whether it resonates with customers in different markets. They can also develop strategies to improve brand recognition and establish a strong presence in the global market.

5) Fostering a culture of innovation: Finally, the leadership team can evaluate it's organizational culture and leadership style to determine how they can foster a culture of innovation within their organization. By encouraging experimentation, creativity, and risk-taking, they can inspire their employees to develop new ideas and approaches to drive growth and success in the global market.

By analyzing it's case study and interpreting the findings for their organization, the leadership team can gain valuable insights into the challenges and opportunities of global expansion and develop a plan to succeed in the worldwide market.

Organizations can use this table to evaluate their strengths and weaknesses in each critical global expansion-related factor. First, they can identify areas where they have a competitive advantage and need improvement. Then, they can develop actionable steps for each weakness, such as investing in employee training to improve language and cultural understanding or conducting market research to understand local consumer preferences better.

The Growth Matrix

Factor	Strengths	Weakness
Reach		
Talent		
Facilities		
Diversification		
Brand Awareness		
Investment Opportunities		

Organizations can then use this information to develop a summary report outlining their strengths and weaknesses concerning global expansion and identifying specific steps they will take to improve their competitiveness in the worldwide market. This report can serve as a roadmap for the organization's international expansion strategy and help ensure they succeed in the global marketplace.

If you are considering expanding your business into international markets, we encourage you to carefully evaluate the potential benefits and challenges of such a move. We hope the information and insights provided in this article have helped guide your decision-making process.

Suppose you have further questions or want to discuss your specific situation more. In that case, we encourage you to contact a qualified professional or consultant like us who can provide personalized advice and guidance. Good luck on your journey toward global expansion!

Mergers and Acquisitions for Growth

"Mergers and acquisitions drive business growth, expanding reach and resources while boosting competitive advantage in today's dynamic environment."

In 2017, I was consulting a multinational corporation in San Jose, California; I had the opportunity to assist them in a game-changing merger and acquisition (M&A) strategy. The company was a significant player in the semiconductor industry and wanted to expand its operations and market share to stay ahead of the competition.

After conducting thorough market research and analysis, we recommended a horizontal merger with a competitor in the same industry. This would allow the MNC to access new markets and customers, increase efficiency and leverage synergies, and build a new business model to help them achieve their goals more effectively.

The M&A process was challenging and required careful consideration and planning to ensure its success. One of the biggest challenges was aligning the cultures and values of both companies and ensuring a smooth integration process.

We worked closely with both companies' executives to ensure the merger would benefit both organizations and create a stronger, more competitive entity. We also navigated the legal and regulatory requirements of the M&A process to ensure a successful outcome.

Despite the challenges, the M&A strategy was a game-changer for the MNC. The merger enabled the company to access new markets, customers, and resources, which resulted in increased profitability and growth.

Moreover, the MNC acquired valuable talent and intellectual property that it may have yet to be able to access otherwise, providing them with a competitive edge in the industry.

Overall, the M&A strategy we recommended and implemented was a huge success for the MNC. It helped them expand their operations and stay ahead of the highly competitive technology industry.

M&A is a powerful strategy that can help organizations to increase their market share, access new resources, and gain a competitive advantage. I share with you the various benefits of M&A and the different types of mergers and acquisitions that organizations can pursue to achieve their goals.

Mergers and Acquisitions (M&A) are an integral part of the corporate world, serving as a means for companies to increase their market share, access new resources, and gain a competitive advantage. In today's fast-paced business environment, M&A has become an essential strategy for organizations to grow and expand their operations and overcome economic and market challenges.

One of the key benefits of M&A is the ability to fill critical gaps in service offerings or client lists. By acquiring or merging with other organizations, companies can access new markets, customers, and resources and improve their competitiveness. This helps companies to expand their reach, reach new customers, and create new business opportunities, which is critical to their long-term success.

Another critical advantage of M&A is the efficient way to acquire talent and intellectual property. Developing the right talent and intellectual property is essential to success in today's competitive environment. By merging with or acquiring other organizations, companies can access a wealth of talent and intellectual property that they might not have been able to access otherwise. This can help companies to gain a competitive edge and to achieve their goals more quickly and effectively.

M&A also allows organizations to leverage synergies, which can help drive growth and improve overall efficiency. By combining the strengths of two or more organizations, companies can leverage economies of scale, reduce costs and increase profitability. This can help organizations to compete more effectively and to grow their business over the long term.

Another benefit of M&A is the ability to build a new business model. By acquiring or merging with other organizations, companies can create a new business model that leverages the strengths of both organizations and enables them to achieve their goals more effectively. This can help companies to stay ahead of the competition and to continue to grow and expand over time.

Finally, M&A can also help companies to save time and avoid long learning curves. By acquiring or merging with other organizations, companies can leverage the experience and expertise of those organizations to quickly gain knowledge and skills that might have taken years to develop otherwise. This can help companies to achieve their goals more rapidly and to avoid costly mistakes that have been made through trial and error.

There are various types of M&A, including horizontal mergers, vertical mergers, concentric mergers, conglomerate mergers, traditional acquisitions, and reverse mergers. Every kind of M&A serves a different purpose and provides other benefits, and organizations should carefully consider which type of M&A is best suited to their needs and goals.

M&A is a powerful tool that can help organizations to achieve their goals, expand their operations, and stay ahead of the competition. By acquiring or merging with other organizations, companies can access new markets, customers, and resources, improve their competitiveness, leverage synergies, and build a new business model. Whether organizations want to grow their business, overcome challenges, or gain a competitive advantage, M & A can help them achieve their goals and reach their full potential.

And there you have it, a comprehensive overview of the benefits and different types of mergers and acquisitions. Whether you want to grow your business, overcome challenges, or gain a competitive advantage, M&A can help you achieve your goals and reach your full potential.

Illustrating through practical examples

One of the most notable examples of a global company that has used M&A as a key growth strategy is the technology giant. It has a long history of pursuing mergers and acquisitions to expand its reach, access new markets, and gain a competitive advantage.

One example of it's successful M&A strategy is its acquisition of open-source software solutions. In 2018, it announced it would acquire this open-source platform for $34 billion, making it the most prominent software acquisition in history.

By acquiring them, this IT giant gained a foothold in the fast-growing cloud computing and hybrid cloud solutions market. This open-source software solutions are widely used in cloud computing, and the acquisition allowed it to offer its customers a more comprehensive suite of cloud solutions.

In addition to expanding ir's cloud offerings, the acquisition also gave access to a wealth of talent and intellectual property. This open source company has a strong reputation for innovation and a deep pool of skilled employees, allowing them to strengthen its technology capabilities and accelerate its growth.

The acquisition also helped them to leverage synergies and improve overall efficiency. The company achieved significant cost savings and improved profitability by combining It's cloud offerings with open-source solutions. The acquisition also allowed them to better compete with its rivals, in the cloud computing market.

Overall, it's acquisition of open-source platform demonstrates the many benefits of M&A, including the ability to access new markets, acquire talent and intellectual property, leverage synergies, and improve overall efficiency. As companies face economic and market challenges, M&A will likely remain a critical growth and expansion strategy.

Take your time and try to answer these questions.

Key questions that a leadership team of an organization might be asked to evaluate their understanding of this case study:

1) What was the main driver behind it's acquisition of open-source solution, and how did the addition help them to expand its presence in the cloud computing market?

2) How did open-source software solutions align with it's existing technology capabilities, and how did the acquisition of open-source solutions allow them to offer a more comprehensive suite of cloud solutions to its customers?

3) What were some of the critical benefits that it gained from the acquisition of this open-source solution, and how did these benefits help them to better compete with its rivals in the technology industry?

4) What challenges did they face in integrating this open source solutions into its existing business operations, and how did they address these challenges to ensure a successful integration?

5) How did the acquisition impact it's overall strategy and future direction, and what lessons can other

organizations learn from it's approach to M&A and strategic partnerships?

How can it work for you?

Once you evaluate this case study and discuss the key questions, a leadership team of your organization can interpret the findings to their organization in several ways:

1) Identifying the key drivers behind M&A activity: This case study highlights the importance of identifying the key drivers behind M&A activity, such as expanding market share, accessing new resources, and gaining a competitive advantage. By understanding these drivers, organizations can evaluate their M&A strategies and determine whether M&A is appropriate for achieving their goals.

2) Assessing the fit between organizations: The case study also underscores the importance of determining the fit between organizations before pursuing an M&A deal. This includes evaluating the compatibility of technology capabilities, corporate culture, and strategic vision and identifying potential synergies and areas of overlap. By carefully assessing the fit between organizations, organizations can minimize the risk of integration challenges and maximize the potential benefits of M&A activity.

3) Focusing on open-source solutions: The case study highlights the value of open-source solutions in the technology industry and how they can help organizations to offer more comprehensive and flexible solutions to their customers. Organizations can leverage the broader

community's expertise and develop more scalable and customizable solutions by focusing on open-source solutions.

4) Balancing short-term and long-term goals: The case study also underscores the importance of balancing short-term and long-term goals when pursuing M&A activity. While M&A can provide significant benefits regarding market share and competitive advantage, it is also essential to consider the potential risks and challenges associated with integration. As a result, organizations can ensure that their M&A activity aligns with their strategic vision by focusing on short-term and long-term goals.

Overall, this case study provides valuable insights into the benefits and challenges of M&A activity and how organizations can approach M&A strategically and effectively. By interpreting the findings for their organization and incorporating them into their decision-making processes, organizations can better position themselves for success in the fast-paced and ever-changing business environment.

Have a measurable and actionable approach to evaluating their current position and making strategic decisions to improve their overall performance. Organizations can use the information to develop a plan outlining the key takeaways and action steps to address weaknesses and capitalize on opportunities.

We hope you found the information helpful in understanding the benefits and different types of M&A organizations can pursue to achieve their goals.

Suppose your organization is considering a merger or acquisition. In that case, we encourage you to carefully evaluate your options and seek the guidance of experienced professionals who can help you navigate the complex process. Additionally, we recommend conducting a SWOT analysis to identify your organization's strengths, weaknesses, opportunities, and threats to inform your decision-making process.

We would happily answer any questions about M&A or provide additional resources to support your organization's growth and success. Please feel free to reach out to us if we can assist.

The Growth Matrix

Conclusion

> *"Just like a seed planted in fertile soil, the growth of an organization begins with a visionary idea. Then, with dedicated nurturing and perseverance, it flourishes into a thriving entity, scaling new heights and leaving an indelible impression on the world."*

Starting a business can be an exciting and rewarding experience, but it also comes with its fair share of challenges. Therefore, it's essential to consider the various aspects of organizational growth you may encounter. From maintaining your company culture to investing in your people and infrastructure, many vital areas require attention to achieve sustained growth over the long term.

During a beautiful summer day in Sydney, I enjoyed indulging in exquisite filo pastries and rice rolls paired perfectly with a freshly brewed cappuccino from Ducale coffee. As I sat enjoying my delectable treats, my mind raced with ideas, and I was on the verge of finalizing my plans to start my startup.

After savoring every last bite, I decided to stroll through the bustling streets of Sydney, eventually finding myself in the charming neighborhood of Bligh Street. As luck would have it, I stumbled upon an available office space and wasted no time booking it.

With that single decision, my entrepreneurial journey had officially begun. The cloudy skies overhead did little to dampen my excitement as I eagerly set to work on bringing my ideas to life in the vibrant city of Sydney. It was a small start-up with just a handful of employees. Everyone wore multiple hats, and we worked long hours to complete everything. As the company began to grow, we faced many challenges.

One of the biggest challenges was maintaining our company culture. As we hired more people and expanded into new markets, keeping everyone aligned with our core values and mission became harder. We also had to adapt our processes and workflows to accommodate the increased volume of work and new stakeholders.

To address these challenges, we invested heavily in our people and infrastructure. For example, we hired an HR manager to help us establish better employee engagement practices and launched a company-wide training program to ensure everyone understood our mission and values. We also implemented new technology and automation tools to streamline workflows and increase efficiency.

Over time, these investments paid off. Our company culture remained strong, even as we grew from a small start-up to a mid-sized organization with hundreds of employees. Thanks to our streamlined processes and talented team, we expanded into new markets and took on more complex projects.

Of course, we faced new challenges as we continued to grow, but we learned that investing in our people and infrastructure was vital to overcoming these obstacles. Our experience taught us that growth could be a double-edged sword, but it can be a tremendous opportunity for organizational success with the right approach and mindset.

As our organization grew, we realized we needed a more strategic approach to managing our expansion. As a result, we began to focus on the following key areas:

We established a long-term strategic plan with specific growth goals, key performance indicators, and timelines. This helped us stay focused on our core objectives and made deciding which opportunities to pursue easier.

Invested more time and resources into our hiring process to ensure we were attracting and retaining the right people. We identified the key competencies necessary for our organization's success and used these as the basis for our hiring process.

It continued to streamline our processes and systems, using technology and automation tools to reduce errors and increase efficiency. This allowed us to handle more volume and complexity without sacrificing quality.

We focused on developing our leaders to help them manage organizational growth challenges. This included providing training and coaching on leadership skills and mentorship and development opportunities.

Communication was a top priority at every level of our organization. We held regular town hall meetings, establishing clear communication channels, and encouraged open and honest feedback from our employees.

We saw significant improvements in our organizational growth as we implemented these strategies. We expanded into new markets, increased our revenue and profits, and attracted new talent. We also saw improvements in our employee satisfaction and engagement, as our team members felt more connected to our company culture and mission.

Of course, there were still challenges along the way. For example, we had to adapt our strategies as the business landscape shifted and make difficult decisions about where to invest our resources. But by staying focused on our core objectives and investing in our people and infrastructure, we overcame these challenges and achieved sustained growth over the long term.

Organizational growth is a multifaceted process involving much more than increasing the company's size. Instead, it involves sustainably expanding the organization's vision and impact, which requires a commitment to change, resilience, and empowering employees to reach their full potential.

Successful organizational growth is not just about the numbers but about creating a culture that fosters innovation, creativity, and adaptability. This means being open to new ideas and ways of doing things and constantly challenging the status quo to find new growth opportunities.

At the same time, building resilience in the organization is essential to weather the inevitable challenges and setbacks of growth. This requires a strong foundation of processes, systems, and leadership to withstand the pressure of growth and change.

Finally, organizations must empower employees to take ownership of their work and develop their skills and knowledge to achieve sustained growth. This involves providing opportunities for growth and development, creating a supportive and inclusive work environment, and recognizing and rewarding employees for their contributions to the organization.

Successful organizational growth requires a holistic approach prioritizing vision, innovation, resilience, and employee empowerment. By focusing on these critical areas, organizations can achieve sustained growth and create lasting impact in their industries and communities.

Why Is It So Important?

Organizational growth is a complex and multifaceted process that involves expanding an organization's size, impact, and vision. According to a report by Deloitte, 75% of organizations worldwide prioritize growth, but only 17% achieve sustained and profitable growth. This indicates that while many organizations recognize the importance of growth, they need help to achieve it sustainably and profitably.

To achieve sustained growth, organizations must prioritize several vital areas. First, they must establish a clear and compelling vision that inspires and motivates their employees—according to a study by Bain & Company, companies with an articulated and well-communicated vision outperformed their peers by 12.4 over ten years.

Organizations must prioritize innovation and creativity to stay ahead of the competition. According to a survey by

PwC, 61% of CEOs worldwide believe innovation is a crucial growth driver. However, only 29% believe their organizations must be more innovative to achieve their growth targets.

Organizations must build resilience in their operations to weather the challenges and setbacks of growth. According to a McKinsey study, companies that could maintain or improve their profit margins during economic uncertainty were more likely to achieve sustained growth over the long term.

Organizations must prioritize employee empowerment and development to create a culture of continuous learning and improvement. According to a report by Gallup, organizations with high employee engagement levels outperform their peers by 147% in earnings per share.

Organizations must also invest in their infrastructure and processes to achieve sustained growth. This includes leveraging technology and automation to streamline workflows, increase efficiency, and invest in talent acquisition and development to ensure they have the right people in the right roles.

However, achieving sustained growth takes work. According to a study by Harvard Business Review, only 10% of organizations can achieve sustained growth over ten years. This suggests that many organizations need help to maintain their growth momentum over the long term.

Organizations must be willing to adapt and evolve to achieve sustained growth. They must be open to new ideas and ways of doing things and ready to challenge the status quo to find new growth opportunities. They must also be willing to make difficult decisions about where to allocate their resources and which opportunities to pursue.

Leadership also plays a critical role in achieving sustained growth. According to a report by Deloitte, organizations with strong leadership outperformed their peers by a factor of 1.5 over ten years. Firm leaders must be able to inspire and motivate their employees while also providing clear direction and guidance.

Here are a few exciting pieces of data of interest:

1. Importance of innovation: According to a study by PwC, 61% of CEOs believe that innovation is a crucial driver of growth, and 82% of CEOs believe that innovation is essential for their organization's long-term success.

2. Role of leadership: A study by Gallup found that 70% of the variance in employee engagement is directly attributable to management. This highlights the importance of effective leadership in driving organizational growth and employee satisfaction.

3. Employee turnover: Employee turnover can be a significant obstacle to organizational growth, as it can be costly to replace talent and can disrupt workflows. According to a Society for Human Resource Management report, the average cost-per-hire is $4,129, and it takes 42 days to fill a position.

4. Impact of technology: Technology can play a significant role in driving organizational growth, as it can increase efficiency, reduce errors, and improve

decision-making. According to a survey by Deloitte, 85% of companies believe that technology is essential for their growth strategy.

5. Customer satisfaction: Customer satisfaction is closely linked to organizational growth, as satisfied customers are more likely to become repeat customers and recommend the company to others. According to a study by American Express, 81% of happy customers are likely to recommend the company to others, while only 19% of dissatisfied customers are likely to do so.

In summary, achieving sustained growth is a complex and multifaceted process that requires organizations to prioritize several vital areas, including vision, innovation, resilience, employee empowerment, and infrastructure. By investing in these areas and being willing to adapt and evolve, organizations can achieve sustained growth and create lasting impact in their industries and communities.

As a thought leader and experienced entrepreneur, I offer leadership coaching, organizational growth coaching, consulting, and mentoring services to help organizations achieve sustained growth. My approach is based on years of experience and the latest research and best practices in organizational growth and leadership development. I am committed to helping organizations achieve their growth objectives sustainably and profitably. If you want to learn more about how I can help your organization achieve sustained growth, please get in touch with me for a consultation.

Sources & References

1. "Global Business Survey 2019: How global businesses are partnering to drive growth" by PwC: https://www.pwc.com/gx/en/services/advisory/deals/global-business-survey-2019.html

2. "Organizational Growth Trends: From Entrepreneurial Start-up to Blue-Chip Behemoth" by Harvard Business Review: https://hbr.org/1989/09/organizational-growth-trends-from-entrepreneurial-start-up-to-blue-chip-behemoth

3. "Growth Trends and Challenges in Today's Organizations" by Deloitte: https://www2.deloitte.com/content/dam/Deloitte/us/Documents/human-capital/us-cons-growth-trends-and-challenges-todays-orgs.pdf

4. "The Challenges of Organizational Growth" by Forbes: https://www.forbes.com/sites/forbestechcouncil/2020/03/11/the-challenges-of-organizational-growth/?sh=4be4dcac6573

5. "Trends and Challenges in Organizational Growth" by McKinsey & Company: https://www.mckinsey.com/business-functions/organization/our-insights/trends-and-challenges-in-organizational-growth

6. Forbes: https://www.forbes.com/sites/davidsturt/2021/06/29/the-leadership-skills-most-in-demand-post-pandemic/?sh=63b6c2425af8

7. McKinsey & Company: https://www.mckinsey.com/featured-insights/future-of-work/what-is-the-future-of-work

8. Deloitte: https://www2.deloitte.com/us/en/insights/economy/industry-4-0/what-is-industry-4-0.html

9. Harvard Business Review: https://hbr.org/2020/03/the-research-is-clear-long-hours-backfire-for-people-and-for-companies

10. Harvard Business Review: https://hbr.org/2021/01/what-the-pandemic-taught-leaders-about-workplace-flexibility

About Author

Rajalingam Rathinam is a distinguished business professional with over 35 years of global experience elevating business success through a comprehensive approach. His expertise in various areas, including organizational growth, branding and marketing, digital transformation, entrepreneurial mindset, emotional intelligence, and ISO 27001 compliance.

As an author, Rajalingam's insights and thought leadership has been featured in several leading business publications. As a result, he is a highly respected figure in the industry, sought after by businesses of all sizes, from startups to multinational corporations.

In his latest book, "The Growth Matrix," Rajalingam presents a strategic framework for achieving business growth and success. The book is the culmination of his decades of experience and expertise, providing a comprehensive guide for business leaders to navigate the complexities of the modern marketplace.

Rajalingam's unique blend of knowledge, skills, and experience has made him a highly sought-after consultant and speaker. He has helped numerous organizations achieve their goals and objectives with his passion for assisting businesses to succeed and his deep understanding of the industry. In addition, his exceptional ability to connect with his clients and inspire them to achieve their potential makes him a valuable asset to any organization seeking to grow and thrive in today's ever-changing business landscape.

www.ingramcontent.com/pod-product-compliance
Lightning Source LLC
Chambersburg PA
CBHW031619210526
45464CB00004B/1653